The 7 Success Habits of Homeschoolers

By Alison Moore Smith

The 7 Success Habits of Homeschoolers
Alison Moore Smith

Published by:

ProSapien LLC

ISBN-13: 9798679305120

Printed in USA

Dedicated to:

Samuel

&

Jessica - Belinda - Alana - Monica - Samson - Caleb

They are everything.

Table of Contents

Foreward

My children are more precious to me than anything. Giving them what they need to reach their potentials is of the utmost importance. I know that's true for good parents all around the world.

But what fits one child, doesn't always fit another—even in the same family—and sometimes it's a real struggle to find the best way to educate each of our children.

In her new book, *The 7 Success Habits of Homeschoolers*, Alison Moore Smith demonstrates a new model for homeschooling. Rather than encouraging a re-creation of school at home, she shows how the flexibility of homeschooling is its greatest asset. Rather than promoting a teaching method, she presents underlying principles. She teaches how a proper vision of homeschooling can lead to a completely individualized education for each child in your family. The perfect kind of education.

Unlike some homeschoolers, she sees value in all forms of education, including the public and private schools. By incorporating homeschooling, public and private schooling, community education, distance learning, apprenticeships, co-ops—and every other resource imaginable—she opens up an incredible array of possibilities. These possibilities offer the best of all options and allow all children to learn in the way that best fits their unique talents.

Whether you are a homeschooling family now, are thinking about homeschooling in the future, or are looking for ways to improve any educational system, this book can act as a cornerstone. It will give you sound steps to sort through the information, data, and sources to hone in on those ideas that will truly benefit your children.

Every child deserves individual attention and an education that addresses their needs, their interests, and their abilities. They need a way to learn that fits them rather than one they are forced to fit. Alison Moore Smith's wonderful new book will show you how to create that kind of learning environment for your whole family.

Richard Paul Evans
#1 NY Times bestselling author of *The Christmas Box*

Introduction

When our homeschooling journey began—entirely against my will—in 1994 I nearly lost my mind. Having been raised in a "normal" family, we all attended public school from kindergarten through high school. We took the required classes, schmoozed the teachers, gamed the system, and aced the standardized tests. Then we set off to prestigious private universities with academic scholarships tucked neatly into our backpacks.

That was the way things were done. And we did it well. It's the only educational model I knew and closely resembled the model my husband was raised with as well. We couldn't imagine anything else.

Yet, there we were, beginning to homeschool our children, embarking on a journey into the fringes of society. And there wasn't a roadmap in site. How did we let this happen?

In a state of sheer panic—and with three weeks to go until the official first day of school—I struggled to come up with a workable plan. Ultimately that "plan" ended up being the re-creation of a mini public school in my home, complete with white board, workbooks, schedules, and even a bell. We stopped short of ordering the 630 Series polyethylene combo desks with ergonomic design, but we were close.

It only took a few weeks of floundering with that model to see the fatal flaw. We weren't in a school and had no need to pretend that we were. But what else could we do? How could "school" possibly look any different.

This was the early internet era, so I turned to books, online forums, and desperate prayer. There were myriad homeschooling methods touted, mostly by those who wanted me to buy their products, or by those who already bought the products and wanted me to assimilate. But every time I researched a new method, I found the same thing: a few good ideas surrounded by flawed reasoning. They might work for some children in some circumstances, but all had fundamental breaking points at which they logically or practically fell apart.

With three kids (that later expanded to six children) I knew I couldn't invest the time and effort into three (or six) widely disparate systems. Still, I wanted to address my children individually and give them the personalized education I thought they deserved.

As I searched for a solution, I finally realized that I didn't want yet another method. I didn't want a new system. There were plenty of both to go around. I wanted a set of underlying principles that would work with every child, in every circumstance—a foundation upon which to build our homeschool, that I could then customize to fit.

For a full year I researched to find what I was looking for. The solution came when I recognized the fundamental nature of some principles I had already incorporated into my life.

Five years before all the homeschooling craziness started, I read a groundbreaking new book titled *The 7 Habits of Highly Effective People* by Stephen Covey. It changed my life. As a wife and mother, it gave me a new way (dare I say a new paradigm?) of looking at my family. As the president of my church's female auxiliary, it gave me a handle on effective leadership. As a business owner, it showed me how to manage an organization. I'd lived by its principles for years and found a solid foundation.

Suddenly it occurred to me that the same principles Stephen Covey created for organizations could also provide a stabilizing groundwork for homeschooling and, indeed, any educational philosophy. So, I set to work modifying the ideas I had learned in The 7 Habits to fit my new world of homeschooling.

The resulting article, "The 7 Habits of Highly Effective Homeschoolers," was published in the July/August 1996 issue of Super Learning Tools. Later, with further adjustments, it became the subject of a convention speech. Today, you're holding the final product of nearly three decades of work, research, and experience: *The 7 Success Habits of Homeschoolers*.

Homeschooling has been exhilarating, exhausting, interesting, frustrating, exciting, and amazing. Here's hoping that this book removes a few of the speed bumps on this wonderful journey with your children. May you have the best homeschooling experience ever!

The 7 Success Habits of Homeschoolers

By Alison Moore Smith

Homeschoolers are Freaks & Weirdos

You came back from the dead to tell me that I'm odd?

Joseph Donelly, *Far and Away*

In 1978 I was introduced to the world of homeschooling by my boyfriend (if someone who is not allowed to date can, indeed, have a boyfriend), Kimball. He was 19 years old, in college, and the eldest of many children. How many, I cannot be sure, since my last contact with him included details of his mother's latest pregnancy. This family was particularly fond of herbs, tax avoidance, long dresses with puffy sleeves, and end-times discussions. Due to the "fact" that "hospital personnel use invisible ink to tattoo social security numbers on babies' foreheads—and that is the 'mark of the beast'"—they were also devoted to home birth.

Kimball tried, at every opportunity, to convince me of the benefits of his alternate version of the American Dream. He also told me that I would be his "first wife."

These were the first homeschoolers I ever met and the reason I tried to avoid homeschoolers for the next decade and a half.

As I matured in wisdom—and turned the ripe old age of fifteen—I came to my senses and ran—fast and far. I found more normal boys with whom to associate (well, usually) and swore that I would never have anything to do with the kooky people in the alternative schooling movement. Ever.

Fast forward.

In 1987 my husband and I had our first child: a beautiful, tiny daughter. We named her Jessica and immediately began filling her life with stimulating, educational pursuits. We did all we could to prepare her to succeed in school.

As her fifth birthday approached, just a few weeks before the beginning of the school year, we pondered aloud the wondrous experience Sandpiper Shores Elementary School would provide for her. It would be fun! It would be joyful! It would be amazing!

Jessica entered Boca Raton, Florida's public kindergarten in August 1992, almost on schedule. True, there was a one-day delay to accommodate the devastation wrought in our neck of the woods by Hurricane Andrew, but we were confident the teachers would be able to creatively make up for that lost time. (They did, by extending the school calendar another day in June.)

As Jessica and I, accompanied by two-year-old Belinda in a stroller, walked to the bus stop that first, fateful day, we were entranced by all the fun that lay in store. She climbed aboard the bus and selected a seat… that was apparently being saved for someone else. She found another that was only for boys. She moved down the aisle and eventually found an empty spot that she was allowed to sit in by the ruling bus matriarchy. She sat down and peered out the window at me. Her eyes barely cleared the edge of the window as she strained to see me. I smiled and waved and blew kisses until the bus was out of sight. Then I bawled my eyes out.

She was so little! We hadn't done all the things that needed doing. I wasn't ready to give her up seven hours a day, 180 days a year, for the next thirteen years—only to give her up to college and adulthood and jobs and marriage and grandchildren. I had lost my baby and I wasn't ready to let go.

But I knew it was for the best. That's what I had been told all my life. That's what I had been told when my dad gently nudged me out from behind his suit coat on my first day in Mrs. Tucker's kindergarten class. And that's what I told my daughter...and myself.

Eventually I adjusted to the schedule and the restrictions. I never quite got used to having her sweet spirit missing from our home so much of the time.

Still, I was determined to be "the good mom," doing all I could to ensure the academic success of my child. That meant being involved. I signed up to be a room mother to provide quarterly parties for the children and run a booth at the PTA carnival. I volunteered as a class aide, doing crucial things like cutting out 4,000 black construction paper fences for the Halloween montage and coordinating donations for the Hanukkah Dreidel Fest and the "Winter Holiday" art project. Next I joined the PTA board as the newsletter editor and then campaigned for a position on the School Advisory Council. I won the election, along with a coveted appointment to the SAC Science Committee.

I was in. The principal, office personnel, teachers, and even the custodian, all knew my name and my face. I would make a difference!

Now and then I faced discouragement. Spending hours in committee meetings, planning and discussing things over which the committee in question had no authority whatsoever, seemed pointless. Being banished to other classrooms so Jessica didn't actually see me helping out at school (as that would be distracting to my daughter and would bring calls of nepotism from parents who wanted nothing to do with the schools) was discouraging. Having a teacher chew up my head and spit it out on a lunch tray when I suggested that vouchers might be a way to deal with the over 200% capacity issue, was disheartening. (It was then explained to me, slowly and clearly, that if we had vouchers, some children would leave the school to attend elsewhere—which I had kind of thought was the point of reducing overcrowding—and would irreparably scar the school system.)

Meanwhile, back in my own daughter's class, her fabulous kindergarten teacher (seriously, she was wonderful), Mrs. Tessler, had recommended Jessica for testing for the gifted program. The gifted program was a magnet school in a "less desirable" area where exceptional children were bussed after being tested either by the school psychologist or by rich parents who had close friends in the psychiatric field. (Percentages in the gifted program suggested that some of the more elite neighborhoods had "really good water" for brain development.)

After some research, the benefit of the magnet school seemed negligible, so we remained in the neighborhood school for first grade. Her new teacher, Mrs. Bruno, agreed to try to provide extra stimulation for Jessica and we thought we could make a go of it.

This seemed to work. Mrs. Bruno was helpful and open. But one day Jessica said math was "just okay," because "it's mostly just coloring." Coloring? My father was a math professor, so math proficiency was not only expected, it was literally our bread and butter. What did coloring have to do with the foundation of all scientific study?

Apparently, Jessica completed her assignments quickly and then spent the rest of the hour coloring the intricate border designs on the worksheets while waiting for the rest of the class. Not to sound like an education snob, but that day I knew that something had to change.

During the summer after first grade, Jessica and her now-two sisters, Belinda and Alana, and I began making weekly treks to the public library. While my children looked for books one morning in late July, I browsed through the small parenting section located in the juvenile library. On the top shelf was a small red book about homeschooling. I laughed a little, remembering that I could have been the preferred wife in a tax-free, whole-foods, homeschooling family. Nevertheless, I quelled the nausea building in the pit of my stomach and picked up the book. I flipped through it casually. After reading a couple of compelling things, I thought the book might give me some ideas for fun, educational, summer and home activities. I decided to check it out. I carefully hid it among all the children's books, ensuring that no one would accidentally see it and confuse me with the crazies who isolate their children from the real world.

There is an unwritten rule in the retail service industry that employees are not to comment on customers' selections or purchases. Noting the caloric value of the molten chocolate cake is forbidden. Chatting about the choice in deodorant brands at checkout is taboo.

The same restrictions should apply to librarians.

When it was finally my turn to check out, I handed the pile of books to the man at the desk. When he worked his way down to the secret volume he bellowed out, "Homeschooling, huh? That's pretty neat, I hear!"

I was mortified and burst into an exposé about my life and my completely rational purpose for checking out this bizarre book.

I then made excuses about the selection to the people behind me in line.

"We do not homeschool! I'm just getting ideas for teaching things to my daughter this summer. Homeschoolers are such weirdos. I'd never homeschool. What about socialization?"

They all looked at me incredulously as I babbled my way out the door. I have rarely been so glad to be safely back in my car.

The next afternoon, while reading under my covers with a flashlight, my daughter walked in on me. "Whatcha reading?" she asked.

I peered out from under the duvet. "Who wants to know?"

"Mom!"

I sheepishly turned the book, just enough for her to read the title.

"Homeschooling? What's that?" she asked as only a seven-year-old can when she has discovered that her parents have gone off the deep end.

"Well, you know how you go to Sandpiper Shores? Some kids go to school in their own houses instead."

"Cool!" she exclaimed. "I guess if you went to homeschool, you'd get more than twenty-two minutes for lunch!"

"Mmmhmm," I looked at her from the corner of my eye." I suppose so."

"I guess if you went to homeschool, you'd go to the library more than once every two weeks."

"Well, yes, but..."

"I guess if you went to homeschool, you'd use the computer more than ten minutes a month."

Off she went with All-the-Reasons-You-Never-Wanted-to-Know-Why-Homeschool-Would-Be-Great. I countered with All-the-Reasons-Why-Public-School-Is-Great-and-Why-Homeschoolers-are-Freaks.

And on it went, through the end of that day and into the next. Approximately every 20 minutes or so, Jessica would pop in to share her latest reason for homeschooling. Due to my husband's untimely business trip out of the country, I was left alone to deal with the crisis. (He has a sixth sense that warns him doom is imminent, like the year he left for Korea on the morning of April 14th, when TurboTax showed we had underpaid by $20,000.) I tried to defend myself, but I could see myself losing my grip.

Jessica wore me down and won match point with, "I guess if I went to homeschool, I wouldn't be so bored."

I hung my head in defeat. My only hope was to wait until my husband found a trans-Atlantic phone line and could slap some sense into me.

Finally, he called.

"Honey! I need you!" I cried. "You won't believe the book I've been reading."

"What book?"

I paused to allow the suspense to build. Sam knew all about homeschoolers, just as I did, and he would be strong for me.

"I checked out a book about...homeschooling..."

I held my breath, waiting for my knight in shining armor to swoop down and carry me off into the sunset of normalcy.

"Oh."

Pause for the other shoe to drop.

"'Oh'? Is that it?"

"Well, if we homeschooled it would be okay, because it would be **you**."

There had to be more. I waited. Nothing. I leaned against the kitchen wall for support. How could I possibly do this?

But how could I not at least try?

A Friendly Warning

Look. I'm not about to tell you this book has a tragic ending. I already said in the very first line how it was my favorite in all the world. But there's a lot of bad stuff coming.

William Goldman, *The Princess Bride*

In proofreading this book, my sweet husband referred to the first chapter and said, "Honey, this is a **lot**."

Indeed, it is.

Coming from a world where government-run school is the only real school, considering anything else—even a charter school or private school—can be an onerous leap.

As someone who actually said out loud, "Leaving the public school system is unpatriotic and selfish!" (since one's duty is in propping up the village), I know that even considering homeschooling can seem radical or even morally wrong.

Rest assured, the mindset shift is the hardest part. **That** is the really big thing. The education itself is elementary (and secondary). Taking charge of education in the home is hard. The schooling is relatively easy.

So, hang in there on this first chapter. Remember that homeschooling is as much an opportunity for the parents to grown and learn as it is for the children. It doesn't have to happen overnight, or even by September 1st. Take things in small doses. You have plenty of time!

Habit 1: Change Your Mindset

Change your thoughts and you change your world.

Norman Vincent Peale

Years ago, I received a call from a frustrated friend. After years of trying to help her children from within the public school system to no avail, she had decided, finally, that their needs would simply never be accommodated satisfactorily. She decided to pull them out of school... at the end of the semester. After hearing not only how little they were actually learning, but also how damaging the environment was to them and how each day merely heaped on more frustration and further reinforced their feelings that they were stupid, I had only one question to ask.

"Why wait until the end of the semester?"

"Uh...so they can finish the whole semester," she answered.

"What will that accomplish?" I asked.

"Well, I'm not ready to start homeschooling yet."

I asked her to list the pros and cons of leaving her children in school a few weeks longer. When my friend did so, the cons were the overwhelming winners. The pros? "The school administrators won't be so annoyed."

Most of us attended public school as children. Most of us intend to send our children there, too, along with the majority of our neighbors and friends. But for many, something happens that makes us wonder if there is a better way. And sometimes the best—or only—solution seems to be homeschooling our children. At least until we can find a better alternative.

While some people plan to homeschool their children long before they even have them and others decide to homeschool after weighing all the available educational options, a large percentage who contact me, make the choice to homeschool out of desperation. Their child has not been served in the traditional school setting and they have finally decided they simply must do something drastic.

Schools aren't optimal for some families for many reasons, such as:

- High Intelligence: children far above the norm intellectually generally need to move more quickly and have more challenging material

- Learning Disabilities: children far below the norm need to have specialized materials/environments and greater accommodation

- Physical Disabilities or Illness: some physical problems may make attending a regular school prohibitive

- Learning Styles: schools tend to work best for those who can sit still for long periods and learn best in a lecture format, even very bright children who learn best in other ways often flounder and are labeled as slow

- Talents & Interests: children who want to learn something very specialized or uncommon will generally not be able to find classes to suit them

- Religious or Racial Intolerance: in some areas this intolerance is blatant and dangerous, in others it forces children to forgo important practices or to separate themselves from particular classmates

- Values Conflicts: many parents find that, more and more, they simply cannot tolerate the moral/political/social agenda that their schools reinforce

- Dangerous Environment: gangs, weapons, drugs, fights are extremely pervasive in some schools and increasingly problematic in many others

- Bullying: having personally endured a decade of bullying in public school, I can attest to the fact that it can take years to undo the damage to kids who are regularly targeted

- Pervasive Cliques: exclusivity is so much a part of most schools (at all ages) as to be almost cliché, but constantly being on the outside, picked last, and locked out of the game can do a number of self-esteem

- Teaching Deficiencies: teacher's unions and tenure situations often make it nearly impossible to get rid or poor teachers and, in a school, your options for particular courses are very limited

- Insufficient Materials: texts and other materials may be outdated or of low quality

- Frequent Moves: some who move frequently due to family circumstances find the social aspects as well as the lack of continuity in schooling to be difficult

- Distance: living in remote areas may make attending a regular school problematic

- Family Crises: serious family disruptions can make it difficult to keep up with a rigid district schedule

- Peer Pressure: influence of other students can be detrimental to learning and behavior if the school environment tends to be negative

- Wasted Time: the logistics of educating so many children lend themselves to inefficient use of time; transportation, lining up, waiting on others, disciplinary issues, assemblies, required activities, announcements, substitute teachers, commercial programs, etc., take vast amounts of time that could be used for actual study

- Powerful Interference: money and power can (and do) corrupt any government school system, when unions, government officials, or those who stand to make money or increase their power have more sway in what is taught and how it's taught, you may not be getting what you are forced to pay for

- Irrational Regulations: when schools are used to control the populace, to make unreasonable demands in the name of safety, the public good, or anything else, the harm done can far outweigh any benefit

- Indoctrination: teachers often see parental input as unwelcome, some have carefully constructed their classrooms to be places to politicize/evangelize their students without your knowledge or permission, you might not be OK with that

When these things interfere enough with education, some parents take action. These desperate parents know that public school isn't working for their child. They know they need to do something—anything—different. Often, homeschooling may seem the only option, so they pull their children out of school, but are not sure where to go from there.

In the example above, after weighing the pros and cons of staying in school, my friend changed her tactic. One day after our conversation, she pulled her kids from school and began homeschooling. She never looked back. And, frankly, that's what most people should do once they decide homeschooling is the right option.

Even if you don't have a plan. Even if you don't have curriculum. Even if you don't have a clue.

The truth is, you have time to figure that out while your children are in a better environment…at home. It won't hurt if they miss a day or a week. You aren't on a fixed 180-day calendar set by the school board. It won't matter if they miss the "transportation unit." (They'll see more transportation in the real world than in twelve years of visual aids.) It won't hurt if they miss the weeks of lessons on coordinating conjunctions. (There are only seven and they can all be mastered in about seven minutes.)

Chances are, they'll start learning even before you get ready to teach them. Take them to the library, check out a pile of books, and let them read while you figure it out. Schedule a trip to the museum or zoo. Buy some art materials. Trampolines are always good, too. Let them relax, rejuvenate, and remember how fun learning can be.

Avoid the Big Three Mistakes

In the process of trying to create a homeschooling plan—something completely foreign—new homeschoolers often make one of three mistakes. Be aware of these pitfalls so you can avoid them as you create your ideal homeschool.

Mimicking the Public School Model

Most homeschoolers weren't homeschooled themselves and most have only one educational model: public school. So, to most of us, the only thing that looks and feels like "school" is whatever looks and feels like **public** school. It is familiar and comfortable—at least more comfortable than floundering in a sea of unknowns.

So, often, a public school model is copied at home to alleviate the fear of completely messing up the kids' lives. At least they won't be any more messed up than we are! And at least no one with kids in public school can criticize our methods.

One friend of mine, a new homeschooler, walked out of her front door with her five-year-old every morning at 7:55. Hand-in-hand, they circled the cul-de-sac back to their own porch. Promptly at 8:00 am, they entered the "school room" door and "teacher" rang a bell. The girl sat in her seat in the kitchen...er..."school room" and "Mrs. Johnson" proceeded to take roll and teach the "class." They marched throughout the day, from subject to subject, right on schedule. Recess and lunch were at predictable times. Then, at the end of the "school day," the "teacher" rang the bell and the morning cul-de-sac tour was reversed, returning "home."

Truthfully, this routine may have been fun (for about a week). And it may have been perfect for **this** little girl. But using such a rigid model as a long-term plan for homeschooling is ridiculously inflexible and unnecessary.

One of the greatest benefits of homeschooling is catering to a few instead of catering to the masses. Rigid schedules with very formal settings often used in large institutions are rarely the most effective educational model for a family with a handful of children. What things about school will really work at home? More to the point, what things won't?

Think outside the school box to see a world of possibilities.

Discarding the Public School Model

For some who have endured particularly negative experiences in a public school—either personally or vicariously through their children—the reaction (or overreaction) can be to utterly remove any semblance of government-funded education.

If school is bad, then it's all bad, and we're having none of it!

Textbooks, schedules, lesson plans, calendars, desks—all are thrown out with the proverbial bath water, with no further analysis.

There is much to learn from decades of trial and error. Don't discard it all without consideration. What things work in school could also work in your home? What could be modified to make a nice fit?

Thinking outside the box should allow us to reach back in the box to grab the tools and techniques that are truly useful to our family. Take the best, leave the rest.

Clinging to the Homeschooling Method du Jour

Some new homeschoolers don't think about the public school model at all. Instead they glean all they can from a homeschooling expert (or two or three). Generally, the "expert" falls into one of these three categories:

1. Someone who homeschools

2. Someone who is selling something to homeschoolers

3. Someone who both homeschools and sells to homeschoolers.

You might be thinking, "At least those people know more about homeschooling than I do!"

These experts will tell you all about the phenomenal new method they are using. They may have only used it for three months. They may have only tried it with one seven-year-old. They may not know your children at all. But they are more excited about their "opportunity" than a first-time network marketer. So, based on their testimonial, you enroll in this month's most popular system. And you commit to follow through, come hell or high water.

Thinking outside the box includes doing the same thing we teach our kids to do: thinking for ourselves. Don't be unduly influenced by adult peer pressure! Do your own research. Use common sense. Choose a method only if it is a reasonable fit for your child and your family.

A More Excellent Way

If we model public school, we lose the great flexibility and most advantages of homeschooling. If we discard all things "schoolish," we miss many great resources and time-tested methods, even those that may best suit our child and our family. If we merely go with the popular flow, we may end up like the person who bases an entire wardrobe on faddish trends and ends up with a closet full of gauchos, hip huggers, and pedal pushers, with nothing substantive to wear.

When you homeschool long enough, you'll see that educational trends, like fashions, recycle—and today we just have a big new crop of educational capri pants, low riders, and skinny jeans. Same old clothes renamed and remarketed with some costly new bells and whistles for you to purchase.

There is a more effective way to educate. It is by being proactive in determining what, when, where, and how we teach. It is by taking responsibility for this very personal analysis. It is by opening up and changing our minds about what "schooling" really is.

But this deep discovery isn't nearly as easy as any of those routines listed above. It takes research, analysis, and trial and error. It requires care and thought and prayer. It requires an open mind. It requires standing up to the clique. It requires you to figure out what is best for your children and your family. It requires seeking out the answers that will be unique to you.

To find this personalized educational system, you must realize that education is not what you think it is. There are two crucial steps to finding what is really is. And they are steps you must take yourself.

Question Everything You Know About Education

Ask yourself what purpose, if any, is being served by particular choices or positions. Think hard about what you assume and the ideas you have accepted. Make each notion stand up to scrutiny before it becomes part of your new educational philosophy.

- Do you need to start at the same time each day?

- Do you need rigid daily and hourly schedules for each subject?

- Do you need to do work sitting at a desk or table?

- Do you need permission to use the bathroom?

- Do you need a blackboard?

- Do you need raised hands before anyone speaks?

- Do you need bulletin boards?

- Do you need worksheets?

- Do you need recess?

- Do you need report cards?

- Do you need standardized tests?

- Do you need to ascertain grade level?

- Do you need to hold school on your child's birthday?

- Do you need to take the summer off?

- Do you need a unit study on seasons, colors, clouds, or modes of transportation?

- Do you need hours daily with age-segregated peers to be socialized?

- Do you need to be around bullies to learn to "get along with all kinds of people"?

Before doing something out of habit or familiarity, before doing anything another homeschooler touts, ask yourself if it makes sense in the context of your homeschool with your children. You will probably decide to use some of the techniques you grew up with. But you will likely surprise yourself to see how many have no value in your home.

Question Everything You Hear About Education

Once it is apparent you are thinking about homeschooling, almost everyone you've ever met will materialize with an opinion. You'll hear raving successes and horror stories. You'll hear praise and condemnation. You'll hear just about as much nonsense from within the homeschooling movement as you will from without. (OK, more from without.) And you'll hear some valuable things from both sides as well.

- Consider all of this incoming information, but do so with a critical ear.

- Do you need an education degree to teach elementary and secondary subject matter?

- Is homeschooling best for everyone?

- Are public schools failing?

- Are homeschoolers succeeding?

- Do you personally need expertise in all subjects to homeschool?

- Does a particular method really produce "statesmen"? What is the evidence? (And what is a statesman, anyway?)

- Are children really innately interested in learning everything they will need to know?

- Is structure coercion?

- Is acceleration preferable?

- Are homeschoolers socially inept? Are public schoolers polite and civil?

- Are homeschoolers deprived of all the typical rites of passage?

- Is parental modeling the most important aspect of education?

- Is isolation to same-age peers an accurate "real world" model?

- Can homeschoolers get into college?

- Is Saxon the best math program? (I'll help you with that one... no!)

Before clinging for dear life to the method used by your next-door neighbor, the guy selling you pricey educational seminars, or **your** local school system, ask the hard questions that will give you perspective.

The more you read, talk, and listen, the more input you will get. And this input can give you a roadmap into the vast unknown. But it will not be useful until you have accepted the somewhat daunting task of filtering through all the muck to get to the gems that will serve you and your family.

No one can do this for you. It's entirely up to you.

For me, this filtering was the toughest part of getting my bearings on our homeschooling journey, but it has also given the greatest return on investment.

Test Before Application

Whenever I hear a new idea that intrigues me—and have asked all the pertinent questions I can come up with—I apply this three-part test to the material before I incorporate it into our homeschool.

Logically Sound?

The idea must be reasonable and rational, or it should be discarded outright. While considering and incorporating the innovative and avant-garde, leave the illogical behind.

A sound idea does not need myriad qualifiers and conditions in order to make it accurate. If it does, it needs more refinement. An example of this comes from a homeschool method popular in some circles. This method is often described in terms of a particularly problematic couplet, "Inspire, not require."

The implication is that children should not be "forced" to do anything, but that the desire to become scholars will gush forth intrinsically from deep within the soul of the correctly educated child. Most perfectly, this desire is "ignited" because the homeschooling parent does the thing she desires her child to do—whilst oozing positive statements such as, "This is so cool!" and "Wow! I love learning about fascinating subjects!"

In short order—seeing the parent enthusiastically engrossed in the activity—the child's unquenchable curiosity will overwhelm her or him and s/he will rush in to eagerly join the activity.

One proponent suggested a parent could energetically read Ivanhoe, wear a waist cincher and hooded gown about the house, join the local LARP group, and then place the book strategically on the coffee table next to the gaming controller. This, the theorist claimed, would entice the child to ignore video games and read the book instead.

Perhaps this would work. I just find it more honest and efficient (and less coercive!) to say, "Hey, guys, we're going to study medieval history. Let's go to the library and pick some books to start. This weekend we can watch A Kid in King Arthur's Court. What other ideas do you have?"

We all know our children are influenced by our behavior. I love to sing, read, debate ethics, and code websites. My husband loves anything technical and most sports. A bunch of our children share those interests, because they have access to them and because we are supportive parents. But, to date, none have become experts in the exact areas in which we show the most interest and spend the most time.

As parents, it is our responsibility to clearly guide our children to those things that will be most helpful to them as adults, whether they are instinctively drawn to them or not.

More times than I can count I've had a conversation very similar to this:

Them: *Inspire, not require!*

Me*: So, you're saying you don't make your kids do anything.*

Them*: That's right! They do whatever they are inspired to do!*

Me*: What do your teenagers do?*

Them*: They study independently for seven hours a day! They are great scholars!*

Me*: Independently?*

Them*: Yes.*

Me*: So, they can do whatever they want?*

Them*: Yes.*

Me*: So how is the seven hours of doing "whatever they want" distinguished from the other 17 hours (when, presumably, they also do "whatever they want" since you don't require your kids do anything)?*

Them*: Well...*

Me*: And, wait, is it the seven hours of doing whatever they want that you call "independent study" or is it the other 17 hours of doing whatever they want?*

Them*: Well, they can't completely do "whatever they want." They have to do educational things.*

Me*: So, you don't require them to do anything, but the things you are not requiring for seven hours have to be "educational things"?*

Them*: Yes, well....*

Me*: And you decide what qualifies as "educational things" and "not educational things"?*

Them: *Mostly…*

Me: *So how is requiring only educational things, actually not requiring?*

Them: *Well, we don't require specific things. They get to choose.*

Me: *From amongst the things you have identified as acceptable school activities?*

Them: *Ah…I guess…*

Me: *Do they choose to do chores?*

Them: *Of course, they have assigned chores. We want them to be responsible.*

Me: *So, you require them to do things outside of school and in school.*

Them: *Um…pretty much.*

Me: *Even though you don't…require.*

After hundreds of similar conversations, it has become clear that "inspire, not require" doesn't mean "inspire, not require." It really means something like: *The kids have to do lots of work, but the parents don't have to be extraordinarily involved in determining exactly how much they are doing in any particular subject. Also, parents need to be positive about what the kids are learning and be examples of continued learning themselves.*

Why didn't they just say so?

I understand the attraction to the couplet. It's clever and memorable. But if it gives a false impression in its brevity—and after decades of discussions, I can tell you it does—it isn't useful or effective.

Another logical problem shows up when a method is espoused without attention being paid to how the method works in the real world. Do the proponents recognize (and verbalize) all the factors that contribute to the outcome?

There is one homeschooling family who raised their children with relatively little academic structure. The result? All their children ended up in Ivy League schools. So, with little thought or analysis, masses of homeschoolers decided this family was the model for academic excellence. To reproduce the Ivy League outcome, they abandoned structure.

The only problem was that they forgot to duplicate (or even notice) other critical elements of the model, such as the fact the family lived in an isolated setting with little distraction. They had access to outdoor activities and ranch work, there were many quality academic resources available, the parents were intellectual models who were bright, inquisitive, and willing to spend hours in educational pursuits.

In other words, they had tons of environmental structure even though they had little specific curricular structure. Families who copied the latter without also implementing the former, did not achieve the same results. When the lack of curricular structure—by itself—produced kids eating Fruit Loops out of the box while watching reruns of Gilligan's Island, some parents were surprised.

Rather than wait until our children are 13 years old without any basic academic skills, let's examine whether our proposed method makes sense at the foundation. That should save both our children and us a lot of aggravation and wasted time.

Align with Your Values?

Sometimes a new method is so appealing that parents will actually jump in and try to retrofit their religious beliefs around it. For example, one of my foundational beliefs about instruction for both adults and children comes from my church. It is, "Teach them correct principles and let them govern themselves." In order to embrace a radical child-led educational model, some of my faith have disregarded the first half of the counsel, the part about the parental duty to teach.

Our beliefs and values should not be at the mercy of our homeschooling method.

What is important to you? How do you believe your life should be lived and your time and resources spent? What do you believe about education? About raising children?

If you must compromise your values—or ignore them all together—in order to incorporate a particular method, idea, or philosophy, it should not be considered. If the method doesn't fit, keep on looking. There are plenty of others to try.

Does the principle fit with your family and current life situation?

When looking at various approaches to homeschooling, there are many variables that play a significant role in how, or if, the approach will be effective.

Family Size & Age

When we began homeschooling, we had a second grader and two preschoolers. When I drafted this book, we had a high schooler, a middle school student, two elementary aged children, a preschooler, and a newborn. What worked for us in the first situation did not work for us in the second, due to the vastly different dynamic.

How many children do you have? How old are they? Will this method, curriculum, or idea work with the ages and range of your children?

Primary Teacher

Is Mom, Dad, or someone else the primary teacher? The most effective method depends a great deal on the teacher and the relationship between the teacher and the student. What works for one teacher, may not work for the other—even with the same child.

Home Situation

The physical nature of your home, location, even the weather, can make a difference in what makes the best use of your resources.

Do you have lots of room or is space limited? Are you settled or transient? Are many resources right at hand? Do you have lots of books? Reference material? Computers? Do you have a home business? Do you have a television or computer? Can you reasonably go outside any month during the year, or are you often confined within the home to avoid extreme weather?

If the method you're considering demands a condition you cannot reasonably meet, it will lead to great frustration. Instead, choose one you can live with.

Neighborhood Environment

How will the surrounding environment impact your homeschooling in light of the specific method you are considering?

If you've decided to invent the Teenage Circadian Homeschooling Method—allowing your 15-year-old to go to bed at 2:00 am, get up at noon, spend a couple of hours to become mentally alert, and dive into serious study at around 3:00 pm—you might have great success. If the public school bus drops off all your child's friends in front of your house at 3:15, you might be in for a struggle.

Is your home isolated or are there many distractions? Do you have access to a great library, museums, and cultural events within a reasonable distance? Are there classes and teams your children can join? What about a local support group with activities for parents and children?

All these can influence your homeschooling choices.

Teaching Style

I hate crafts—so much that my husband has dubbed me part of the "anti-craft." In my twenties, a women's church group I presided over changed my title from Relief Society President to "President of the Craft Idiots Club." Yes, I'm that bad.

But for the sake of my more creatively inclined children (weep, sob!) I ventured into the valley of the shadow of crafts. One day I proudly announced to my children that we were about to learn the crucial life skill of papier mâché! We tore up newspaper, mixed up paste, and blew up balloons. We worked for two days on an enormous object. I don't recall what it was, as I'm still suffering from PTSD and partial amnesia over the incident, but I believe it involved farm animal shapes. I also know it included the slimy goo that ruined our new dining room chairs, a couple of shirts, and my bangs.

I determined then and there that I am **not** a messy project person. If I was going to survive homeschooling, it would have to be on terms that both my children and I could live with. And without papier mâché.

Some of them still love messy projects. They just do them at a neighbor's house.

Learning Style

Children, too, have their own preferences. The more children you have, the more flexible you will need to be to find an optimum educational model.

When my oldest, Jessica, was two-and-a-half, she begged me to teach her to read. I put it off, reminding her she would learn in school. I had already been told that some teachers in her soon-to-be school were not pleased with parental "interference."

Finally, a few weeks before she turned five, she wore me down. Having no experience (or interest) in homeschooling, my curricular choices came mainly from infomercials. I bought *Hooked on Phonics* because it was the only program I had ever heard of.

As boring as the reading program was, it worked. Soon Jessica was whizzing through books. In kindergarten she stunned her teacher with her homemade books and perfect spelling. In first grade, while her peers were memorizing whole language "sight words," she was sent to read aloud to the kindergartener classes. There, the students were told that if they worked hard, they could "read just like Jessica." (Never mind that Jessica was taught to read with the "antiquated" phonics method and they were learning to read with the cutting edge labeling of every inanimate object in the classroom where they were expected to memorize the word shapes. I'm sure it made no difference as long as they "worked hard.")

By second grade, she was devouring classics like *Little Women* and *The Lord of the Rings* (no, please, not abridged). Once we thought it charming to buy her the first five-book set of the American Girls books on a trip to Costco. But when she finished reading them **all** just as we drove into our driveway, we realized we should have just checked them out at the library.

A few years later—and after being entrenched in homeschooling— our second child, Belinda, turned five. We figured it was high time she embarked on the wonderful journey to literacy, so we pulled out the *HOP* and got to work. She was certainly capable, but Mother couldn't seem to endure the process. As Jessica had scurried through from beginning to end, "...mat, pat, bat, cat, fat, sat..." Belinda felt each word had a life of its own.

"Mat. We have a mat on our front porch. Remember when the wind blew it down the street and we couldn't find it?" Mom points to the next word.

"Pat. I got to pat the goat at the petting zoo. It ate Jessica's ribbon right off her hair. That was so funny! [Gales of laughter, lasting two to four minutes.] Can we get a goat some day?" Mom points to next word.

"Bat. That's like a bat that flies in the sky at Halloween and it's sooooooo scary. It makes you scared and you hide and you don't want to get a bat to chase you, 'cause they're kind of creepy and they might get you. They have them at the museum, don't they, Mom? Or is it a bat you hit a ball with? Like when we went to the park with Daddy and it was really hot and that boy pushed me in the fire ant pile and they crawled all over my arms..."

Making no progress, we put *HOP* away and let Belinda talk and sing and bounce. Every few months we reintroduced the program, with little progress. She was more interested, motivated, and focused on creating and building things. Once she made an amazing "hat factory" with every kind of haberdashery imaginable. Later she began creating elaborate costumes: alligators, monkeys, dragons with pieces that covered every inch, head to toe, of Alana's body. Her little sister was the perfect model for her creations.

One day, after spending a few hours in her workshop (also known as the garage), she came out utterly frustrated. Unusual for this generally happy, playful girl, I asked her what was wrong. Furrowing her brow, she looked at me with great sincerity.

"Mom, you know the guys who made [Disney World's] Big Thunder Mountain?"

"Yes."

"Well, they must have had a lot of stuff in their garage!"

Only a few days later—after another frustrating afternoon trying to create theme-park rides from empty tuna cans, milk jugs, egg cartons, and other bits and pieces—Belinda burst into my room again. Now halfway through second grade, she declared, "Mom, I just can't make all the things I want to without being able to read the directions."

She began Hooked on Phonics in earnest and with a purpose of her own. Within less than two months, she was reading well past "grade level."

Trying to fit a program or schedule or curriculum to a child rarely works as well as the converse. Whenever possible, work with your child's amazing abilities, not against them.

Proceed with Questioning

There will always be new books, new methods, and new alternatives to analyze. Some of them may fit, most probably won't. Before implementing an idea, take due diligence to first think it carefully through.

As you continued on your homeschooling journey, keep revisiting the questions, asking whether your positions are still sound. This process of questioning is never done.

Final Thoughts

Changing your mindset is the key to having a successful homeschooling journey.

Where you are today is the perfect place to start. You don't need a special degree or certificate or expertise. You need a willing heart, an open mind, and a deep love for your children. The rest of the pieces will fall into place along the way.

Keep thinking. Keep reading, Keep wondering. Keep analyzing. Keep questioning.

For resources and downloads relating to Habit #1, go to:
https://the7successhabitsofhomeschoolers.com/habit1

Habit 2: Define "Well-Educated"

Education is not preparation for life; education is life itself.

John Dewey

L et's assume, for the sake of argument, that you have chosen to ho- meschool because you believe it's the best way to give your children a great education. You're not doing it to spite your mother-in-law, to show up your nosey neighbor (who happens to teach at the local public school), to be a martyr, or to shelter your children from "the real world." You actually just want to give them a high-quality education.

Have you determined what a "high-quality education" is? What does a well-educated child look, sound, and act like? What does she know? What can he do? How does she or he differ from a child who is not "well-educated"?

You must determine the goal. You cannot plan to give your children something you cannot yourself define. A passage from Lewis Carroll's *Alice in Wonderland* addresses this beautifully:

"Would you tell me, please, which way I ought to go from here?" Alice asked.

"That depends a good deal on where you want to get to," said the Cheshire Cat.

"I don't much care where—" said Alice.

"Then it doesn't matter which way you go," said the Cat.

"—so long as I get SOMEWHERE," Alice added as an explanation.

"Oh, you're sure to do that," said the Cat, "if you only walk long enough."

If your homeschooling goal is just to end up **somewhere**, you can skip this step all together. Better yet, skip them all. As long as your heart keeps pumping (and I assume it will), you're bound to end up somewhere.

Similarly, if your goal is for your children to reach adulthood while still breathing, go ahead and pull out the candy corn and licorice. You can sit by and watch your children turn 18 without much more than a few thousand meals and a modest shelter. Your children will, most definitely, end up somewhere (or other). You'll reach your goal!

If, on the other hand, you have higher (or at least different) aspirations for your children, keep reading. Then ask yourself just where your homeschool is headed. If it stays on its current course, where will your children end up? Is that destination acceptable? Desirable? Reasonable?

What Is Success?

Unless you know the destination, you can't tell if your methods and roadmap are getting you closer or not. You cannot evaluate the success of an educational model unless you know where you intend to go with it—unless you know what "success" is. You must begin with the end in mind.

What does success look like to you? At the end of the high school road, what will be an acceptable outcome?

I have a friend who has four children. She used to say, "I just need one lawyer, one doctor, and one accountant. The other one can choose what he wants to do." While this plan won't work out for most of us, at least she had a success model to shoot for!

What is your model? What is your goal? What do you want your children to be when they grow up and move out into the world?

- Self-reliant

- Emotionally agile

- Honest

- Creative

- Empathetic

- Assertive

- Competent for employment

- Entrepreneurs

- Service minded

- Politically active

- Religiously faithful

- Happily married

- Loving

- Academically advanced

- Musical

- Confident in public

- Athletic

- Responsible

- Students at a good college

- Students at an elite college

- Students on a scholarship

- Solid providers

- Creative problem-solvers

- Independently wealthy

- Leaders

- Independent thinkers

What do **you** hope for your children?

As a homeschooling parent, **you** are the foundation. **You** determine the agenda. And you can take action toward that end. Or you can wander from day to day, letting life happen. It's your choice. If you don't make conscious choices, your path will be set by default.

Specify where you want to go and then determine a course of action that will reasonably move you toward the desired outcome.

General, Flexible, Long-Term Goals

To set a course to your chosen finish line, you must determine what actions will get you there. What basic skills, knowledge, attitudes are most likely to lead where you want to go?

Write down these ideas as a set of **general, flexible, long-term goals**—not as a finely-honed set of specifics. When setting the course for the life of **another** person (your child), you must provide an objective that allows many ways to personalize along the way.

Do you value music education? Suppose you set a long-term goal for your child to **attain a reasonable level of musical literacy**. That kind of open-ended goal can be accomplished in myriad ways. Some possibilities include:

- Sign up for four years of classical violin studies with nationally renowned violinist Antionette Benjoli-Pantoon

- Sign up for four years of classical violin studies with a teacher that clicks with him or her

- Sign up for classical, bluegrass, or pop violin lessons with a local coach

- Allow them to choose any instrument that they are interested in and study it to proficiency

- Learn music theory and try a variety of instruments for possible further study

- Play in a garage band

- Learn to read music and obtain sight singing skills

- Study a variety of eras and musical composers; listen to their works and be able to identify similarities and differences

- Compare different music production methods used by your child's favorite groups

- Study music production and digital audio techniques

There are so many paths that can lead to completing a broad goal! How many more can you think of? When your goals are general and flexible, it's easy to find a path that fits your particular child. The possibilities are almost limitless.

When your goals are rigid and specific, you leave little to the imagination and no room for the child to incorporate their own passions and skills.

Decide what general goals are important to you and write them down.

Course Adjustment

Getting the ship on course is not a one-time event. You must continually revisit the map and ask the pertinent questions.

Still On Track?

Over time you may find that you have veered off course. Perhaps a crisis, illness, or other life situation got in the way. Maybe your child had a difficult year and studies became secondary. It could be that you got very involved in unexpected activities that took extra time.

In the time we've homeschooled, we've built three homes. Each building experience has been an education in itself, but also a distraction that required some readjustment. I also had three more babies with more adjustments.

Whatever the reason, if you've gone far from your original plan, see if it is time to turn back to your original goals.

Better Ways?

Our fourth daughter, Monica, had followed Alana with a passion for musical theater. With her sophomore year in high school completely planned, we learned of a new charter school opening nearby. The flagship Pioneer High School for the Performing Arts was opening five miles from our home, with the auditions only a few days away.

This was a school to be headed by working professional performers with a focus on leading the selected students to a career in the arts. To make it even more enticing, the administrators were open to having her enroll only in the performing arts classes while continuing all her academic courses at home.

We quickly pulled things together. She auditioned, was accepted, and spent the next three years with the most amazing vocal, dance, and theater instructors imaginable.

This sudden opportunity drastically changed her planned schedule. It also changed her life and her future career. And the change was perfect for her.

Shifted Goals?

One of the most important reasons to revisit your goals regularly is to determine whether or not the goals are still applicable and reasonable. We learn, we grow, we change our minds. Life circumstances change as well.

Keep your goals and preferred outcomes open for reinterpretation, revision, and even removal. If they no longer fit, adjust as needed!

Child's Input!

As your children grow, develop, and experience life, they will develop more and more of their own interests and passions.

Look vigilantly at their interests, skills, and desires. Incorporate those not only into their daily activities, but also as an integral part of the final goals themselves. **Work with them!** Become their educational allies. When they are truly adults, they will be ready to pursue their own dreams.

Final Thoughts

If you want the end result of homeschooling to be more than a random accumulation of aimless hours, you —as the principal, curriculum advisor, and teacher—will need to have a plan. You need to know the destination. You need to specify the goals.

This plan doesn't have to be rigid and it shouldn't be made without the child's needs, interests, and abilities included as an integral piece of the puzzle. But you must decide what a quality education looks like and how to measure the results, if you are to reach that end.

Decide what it means to be "well educated," and take action toward that result.

For resources and downloads relating to Habit #2, go to:
https://the7successhabitsofhomeschoolers.com/habit2

Habit 3: Organize & Prioritize

Organize yourselves; prepare every needful thing; and establish a house, even a house of prayer, a house of fasting, a house of faith, a house of learning, a house of glory, a house of order, a house of God.

Doctrine & Covenants 88:119

I grew up in an immaculate home. It truly was a "house of order." I don't know how my mother did it—it all has a mystical quality to me—but I do remember watching her iron. All. The. Time.

Truth is, my mother had a once-per-week housekeeper much of my life. She didn't work in the family company. She had a home and yard about half the size of mine. (When I originally wrote this book, our house was four times and our plot of land 20 times larger than the home of my youth!) She didn't homeschool. Most significantly, she had half as many children as I do and they (we) were out of the house approximately 1,200 hours every year.

Most of you have similar comparisons to those you know who live in glass castles. So, it's no wonder we all live like slobs. Right?

I say wrong.

Should homeschooling be an excuse to live a chaotic life? I don't think so. It may be harder to achieve a sense of order and cleanliness with your entire brood home all day long. But it's worth the extra effort. We simply don't learn or live as well in chaos. Order makes for better living and better homeschooling.

The key to having an organized home and life is creating effective systems for your home. Design a system to address each basic home management area within your purview. A sound system must be:

1. Efficient

2. Thorough

3. Predictable

4. Streamlined

5. Personalized

I have devised six home management systems—one for each area of our home that caused stress—to bring order from chaos. To create these systems, I drew on the wisdom of my parents and friends, industry experts, and lots of trial and error. I took the systems of others and massaged them until they fit me and fit my family. I sincerely suggest you do the same personalization.

My way is not the only way! Figure out what works for you—and what won't. Make it a custom fit. Do your research. Practice and modify, until you find a workable system for **you**.

Next, involve your children. My children understand that homeschooling is a privilege—one that uses resources. Therefore, in order to enjoy that privilege, they must be willing contributors to the household.

These life skills are a critical part of being a self-reliant adult and add to a superb education.

Below are the six systems that I use. Modify to suit.

System #1: Physical & Digital Information

The system I use to organize information is a tweak of that taught by David Allen in his groundbreaking book *Getting Things Done*. Get his book. It's a full-fledged course on getting a handle on all the things you need to do. Consider this section a tiny primer.

The information system organizes the notes, schedules, calendars, papers, mail, and minutia in your life. It keeps you on top of what you need to be doing, where you need to go, with whom you need to speak. It's a system that can clear your head for more important things—like geometry proofs and ancient Greek timelines.

At the root, the system really consists of just two steps: capturing incoming information and processing the captured information.

If you have items coming in electronically as well as physically, you'll need a way to capture both kinds of information. If you ever leave your home, it will help to have portable systems that aren't too cumbersome.

Capture Information

To use this system, follow a regular, consistent pattern to keep things from falling through the cracks.

First, gather all the incoming items (mail, email, notes, calendars, invitations, bills, receipts, etc.) into a central location. On my desk, I use a metal inbox basket. On my computer desktop, I use a folder titled "Inbox." Easy enough?

Process Information

At least once a week, I go through each item I have captured and process it appropriately. By that I mean that I get it out of my inbox and determine what should be done with it. If I can do the needed action quickly (in two minutes or less) it gets done right at the time of processing. Other things get put into my action system to be addressed later. Below are my actions systems and some examples of what should go there.

- **Calendar**: Appointments, birthdays, and scheduled events

- **Tickler File**: A calendar for physical items related to a particular date; football tickets, wedding invitations, notes for a meeting

- **To Do List**: Things to do, untimed reminders, repetitive tasks

- **Next Action Folder**: Bills to pay, forms to fill out, lists of all actions

- **Address Book**: Names, addresses, phone numbers, personal info

- **Reference Files**: Anything I need to keep, but don't need to access regularly; tax forms, paid bills, insurance information, loan documents, report cards

- **Someday File**: Things that I may want to access later, but cannot decide yet; symphony season brochures, vacation advertisements, catalogs

- **Delegate File**: Reminder notes for any action items that have been delegated to someone else and need to be followed up on later

- **Project Notebook**: Any action items that take more than one step; family reunions, building a house, buying a car, planning a dinner party; writing a book

- **Outbox**: Outgoing mail or things that need to be delivered elsewhere

- **Trash**: Everything I don't really need

System #2: Long-term Possessions

A place for everything and everything in its place. Unless there is an identified location for things to reside, you have no chance of getting them there. This is reminiscent of the *Alice in Wonderland* situation again. Without a home, scissors are just as "put away" on the couch or in the bathtub as anywhere else. With a specified home, everyone can find them as needed **and** put them away when done.

Organizing is probably one of my favorite activities. While I wasn't born organized, once I learned how, the results were so positive that I could never go back. In fact, when I am pregnant, it is actually a prime outlet for the nesting hormone. I'd sooner sort out a closet or redesign my file system than engage in almost any popular leisure activity. (Not hyperbole.)

I realize that qualifies me for a life knitting red hot pads in a safe room. For the rest of you, here's a step-by-step guide to organizing your space.

Organize Yourself

Tackle your own space first. Don't clean up your husband's act until you've cleaned up yours. Don't start tearing into your daughter's room when you've got clothes from high school (two sizes too small) in your closet.

Start Small

Don't empty out all the cupboards in the game room and try to dig your way out. Start with a drawer or a purse or a shelf. Start with a space that won't take too long and won't leave a tsunami behind you. Trust me here. If you don't, you'll be sorry.

Be Reasonable

Repeatedly I've heard organizing "experts" advise clients to get a big box and put in everything that hasn't been used in the past six months. They are then instructed to tape up the box and place it in the corner of an attic.

"After six months, if you still haven't needed the items, throw them away without looking in the box."

This may reduce the number of things in your home, but trashing everything you haven't used in the past six months isn't sound advice.

Any of you have Christmas decorations? What about a fire extinguisher?

Remove Clutter

Has anyone ever accused you of being a packrat? Of hoarding? Of saving too many things? These are not compliments regarding your frugality! These are signs that you need to take action (or get psychiatric help).

There are so many reasons to eliminate junk, remove debris, and clean up your act. Your junk uses up your valuable space! You pay for that space. You have to clean the junk, clean around the junk, dig through the junk to find what you really want, explain the junk to anyone who drops by, and apologize about your junk to your friends. This is a waste of your time, your energy, and your life.

I know this in a very personal way.

In spite of the fact that I teach this organization, I'm definitely not perfect—and neither is my home. My skeleton is, literally, in my closet. Here is what I wrote about my closet in 2007:

I have a huge walk-in closet. It's bigger than my first bedroom. And it's full, to the brim. It's filled with clothes—maternity and not—in at least four sizes. It has hats I wore in the 1980's and two jewelry boxes full of my mother's and grandmother's costume jewelry. It has hundreds of tee shirts from all over the world, and shoes that I bought in the early 1990s but have still never worn.

The realization that I had a "problem" came to me when Jessica was a junior in high school. She had been cast in a production of the musical Footloose and was looking for costumes. Upon learning that the show was set in the 1980s, I invited my daughter to do a little browsing in my ageless, timeless wardrobe.

She found some jeans I was holding onto, ankle-length, peg leg, acid washed, and with a waistband where one's waist actually resides. So cute! And in great shape. I'm sure I'll fit in them again some day.

She grabbed them. "Oh! They're mom-pants!"

I have no idea what that means, but qualifying anything with the word "mom" must be good.

When she wore them to dress rehearsal, the costume designer screeched. "Those are the ugliest pants I have ever seen in my life!"

It was then I realized that even if I did fit in them again, those jeans were so out of style that I would embarrass the children by wearing them. I had to admit this applied to a large percentage of my retained wardrobe.

Can someone please call "What Not to Wear" and get
me a spot on the show?

Many of us struggle with letting go. But the mental clarity and peace that come from reduce physical chaos is worth it. Below is my own clutter removal system.

Five Boxes and a Bag Organizing Method

To begin you will need:
1 large garbage bag
5 large cardboard boxes (labeled: DUMP; GIVE; PUT; KEEP; EW)
Here is the method of use:

Box #1: Dump Box

Take everything out of the drawer (or cupboard or shelf) and put it in the Dump Box. Everything. Don't fret about it, don't reminisce over it, don't even look at it. Just dump it all straight into the box.

Now thoroughly clean out the empty drawer (or cupboard or shelf). Spic and span. Spotless. You're less likely to junk up a shiny, clean drawer.

Now you will pick up each item in your Dump Box, one at a time, and decide which of the following containers it goes in. You'll continue picking up items until the Dump Box is empty.

Trash Bag

First things first. Throw away the garbage! Anything broken, un-usable, worthless, spoiled, or expired. In the bag. Now. Just do it. Don't clutter up your life with trash!

Box #2: Give Box

Be ruthless! If you can't use it or won't use it, but it's still useful, give it to someone who can and will. Bless the lives of others. Take a tax deduction. Give yourself some breathing room. Everyone wins.

Box #3: Put Box

If you find something that you want and need, but it doesn't belong in the drawer (or cupboard or shelf) you are working on, put it in the Put Box (as in "put it away") to sort through **later**.

Do not put it away now! This is critical! If you are reading this chapter, then you must listen! I know your type! If you pick up that spool of thread and wander to the laundry room to put it by the sewing machine, you will never return. You will see a shirt that needs a button sewn on and you'll start to thread the needle, but you'll remember that the scissors you need are by the ironing board. You'll go to the ironing board only to notice that you forgot to iron your skirt for tomorrow. You'll start to heat the iron and then you'll recall that you are wearing the skirt to a presentation, but haven't finished your presentation slides, so you'll dash to the to finish them, only to see the bills on your desk that need to be paid and...

It will never end. We will never see you again. (My husband is this person. I know you!)

So, like I said, put the thread in the Put Box and slowly...back...away.

Box #4: Keep Box

This box is for the things you use, need, want, and that actually goes back in the drawer (or cupboard or shelf) you just emptied. Don't put it away just yet. Just put it in the Keep Box to be organized later.

Box #5: Emotional Withdrawal Box

Ah, the final box. This is for all that stuff for which you have no good use, that you can't justify keeping, that you do not need, but for some inexplicable reason, you **cannot** bear to part with either.

Remember, this is a high-level condition. If you're honest with yourself and committed to an organized life, there should not be many things that qualify.

I have a few of these things myself. I admit it. Like my fluffy lavender float gown that reminds me I reached my childhood dream of wearing a poofy dress and a tiara and waving to the crowds on the 4th of July from a parade float. And my turquoise pageant shoes, which serve as proof that I did, indeed, win swimsuit competitions back in the day.

These things are of no use, but I will never let them go. Instead, I pack them carefully and put the box in an unneeded corner of the basement, the attic, or (better!) my parents' house. It doesn't get in the way, and I can still keep my treasures.

The Emotional Withdrawal Box is also the means to repay your children for all the teen angst they poured upon you. Some day, after you die, one of them will come across this box of meaningless junk. She will either have to store it in a corner of her own home or throw it away herself and live with that guilt for the rest of her natural life.

Unfortunately, you won't be around to see this unfold, but you can be content knowing it is coming.

Organize It Away

Once your Dump Box empty, it's time to organize everything in your Keep Box. Use these ideas for easy setup and staying power.

Use Containers to Divide and Conquer

Have you ever put a bunch of items in a drawer and then shut it? What happens? Everything slides all over the place. Instead of that kind of mayhem, divide the space to accommodate your things. You need nothing fancy. Inexpensive plastic containers from a dollar store, jewelry boxes or show boxes, even cleaned TV dinner trays can be used to divide the space for your items.

Most of the time I like squares and rectangles, as they waste less space. Containers should have flat bottoms (so the contents don't tip over and jumble). If you need to stack boxes or want to cover the contents, look for containers with attached lids. The lids won't get lost and broken, leaving you with half a container to work with.

Easy In; Easy Out

I'm sure you never leave anything where it shouldn't be. But if you expect your family members to help keep things tidy, make it easy on them. If an item can be put away in one step, it's more likely to be put away than items with more steps. If your kids can toss blocks in a bucket, they might do it. If they have to open a closet, take out a step stool, climb up and reach down a container, open the latch, remove the lid, put the blocks away—and then reverse the entire process—I'll bet you will be stepping on Legos until your last child is 13.

If something is used a lot, store it in the easiest place to reach. Prime storage space is from the knees to an easy stretch above the head. Don't use this space for the Christmas mugs. Use it for the everyday items.

It's easiest to get and replace things that are only one level deep. If you never use that tiny mixing bowl because you have 17 children and a couple of foreign exchange students living in your home, do not nest that bowl on top of the ones you do use. I know they are a set and they'll be sad if you separate them. Do it anyway. They'll get over it.

Same rules apply to storing things deep in cupboards. Put the things you use most in front and lesser-used items behind.

First Use

There is a tendency for humans to store things by category and often this makes sense. But most of the time it's more important to store things where they are used.

My boots are items of clothing, but I don't store them by my underwear. I store them in the mudroom by the garage door, because I only wear them to go outside.

Most of my kitchen utensils are in the two drawers on either side of my cook top. But where do you use a peeler? I don't peel potatoes over the open gas flame, so the peeler is stored in the drawer right next to the sink where I actually peel.

By a raise of hands, how many of you only store toilet paper in the pantry, next to the paper products? Exactly. You keep the rolls where they are first used, next to the toilet.

Think about categories of items, but then think about where you actually use them, and store accordingly.

Duplicate

After harping on you to rid yourself of all the excess, it may seem counterintuitive that I'm telling you to buy more stuff. But I am.

If you have more than one bathroom, you have more than one roll of toilet paper in your house. The same logic applies to many things that are used, repeatedly, in different parts of the house.

We have scissors in each office, the homeschool room, the laundry room, the gift-wrapping center, the kitchen, the garage, and the workshop. We have tape, screwdrivers, pencils, and paper in all sorts of places. Back in the day of the land line, we had phones throughout the house. Oh, and televisions.

Make these items convenient. If you don't, they'll never be where you want them, because they'll be moved to another location of use and won't find their way back.

System #3: Home Cleaning & Maintenance

As a disclaimer, I am well aware that women and men are capable of doing housework. For the record, I teach my boys the same home management skills I teach my girls. My own father—and my husband—contribute at home, even while taking the more traditional role (should that be roll?) of primary breadwinner.

However, about 90% of those who attend homeschooling conventions where I speak are women. Even higher percentages are the main homeschool teachers in their homes. I'm addressing the cleaning issues primarily to women simply because they are the primary homeschooling audience. If you're a man, the systems still apply.

Organizing and cleaning are utterly distinct activities, although the former greatly facilitates the latter. While I do not enjoy cleaning, I love a clean space and function better in one.

To me, the purpose of cleaning is to get it done as efficiently as possible, so that real life can continue in a positive environment. Thus, I've searched for methods that are the most efficient. When I approached cleaning as a professional and created a plan of action, I got the best results in the least amount of time.

There are two parts to this plan: what to clean and how to clean it.

What to Clean

Weekly Schedule

Create a weekly schedule. Decide what day you will you dust, vacuum, disinfect bathrooms, etc. Include things like errands and shopping on the schedule as well. You won't be doing much cleaning on Tuesday if you are gone all day long. Writing it all down gives you an aerial view of the landscape. You can better see where to fit all your tasks into the week.

Master To-Do List

Next you're going to create a massive list. Write down everything that you ever need to do to keep your home clean and functioning. Yes, this includes dusting and mopping. It also includes changing the air conditioning filters, cleaning out the gutters, and filling the water softener with salt. If you're lucky, it includes cleaning the pool filter. (OK, if you're really lucky, you'll have a pool boy do that, but it's all relative.)

Add to this list all the things you do repeatedly, even if they aren't really connected to the home itself: dentists' appointments, oil changes, writing Christmas cards.

Determine Frequency

Now determine a frequency for each of the items on your list and write it next to the item. Auto registration would be renewed annually and your towels washed weekly, for example.

Record

If you're doing this digitally, enter each item into a digital to-do list with a solid repeating function. Give each one a start date (based on the day appropriate day of the week) and appropriate repetition.

If you're doing this manually, copy each item on your list onto a 3x5 card, with the frequency listed in the top corner. Fill a recipe box or shoe box with tabbed dividers for each month and the numbers 1-31 in a recipe file box. File each card behind the next date to do it.

When you complete a task, check it off or move it to the next date it needs to be done.

How to Clean

Our homes are filled with so many surfaces. Effective cleaning is more complicated than ever. You need:

Proper Tools

Have you ever noticed how often men will spend an arm and a leg on a tool—a chop saw or a bench sander—that they will use only once or twice a year on hobby work?

The same weekend warriors will often balk at the idea of investing in just-above-builder grade appliances. While vacuum cleaners, dishwashers, and washing machines are used **daily**, too often those purchases are where the scrimping occurs.

That is not OK.

These items are not luxuries. They are the tools of homemaking. It's worth it to get the best quality you can afford with a feature set you need. Your efficiency will soar when you're no longer saddled with mediocre equipment.

Head to an independent testing source such as *Consumer Reports*, to find the greatest utility and durability, for the lowest cost. You won't be sorry when you spend only half the time getting things twice as clean.

Proper Solutions

Today's homes have wood, leather, tile, stone, paint, fabric, plastic, cement, glass, and more. Each surface requires a different cleaning solution and method. Take the time to learn the best products to use on the surfaces you have. Check with the installer, manufacturer, and cleaning product labels.

Then head to the nearest janitorial supply house and get professional solutions. You'll save money with the concentrated formulas and the results will be better.

Efficient Methods

Ever wonder how a cleaning service gets in and out of a huge office building so fast and leaves it shining? They use the best tools and solutions and the most efficient methods at every step. You can easily apply the same methods to your home.

I like the two-pass system. I carry all the cleaning materials with me and work my way around the room. I start by the door and clean everything, top to bottom, as I work my way back around to the same door. Then I take a second pass to clean the floor. In and out. Done.

System #4: Meal Planning & Preparation

Confession. I have deep disdain for many traditional domestic activities, cooking being high on my list of things to avoid. Still, my family annoyingly insists on eating. I had to come up with a way to accommodate this desire, while following the basic tenets of kitchen management that I hold dear. Alison's Kitchen Rules are:

Be Speedy

Whatever it is, it has to be quick. From conception and creation through consumption and clean up, it has to absorb an amazingly short amount of time in my day.

Be Spartan

It's got to be cheap. I'd rather spend my money on important things like emeralds or silver mesh drawer organizers. Or cruises to the Caribbean. I don't want to spend a lot on something that will be consumed within minutes.

Be Salubrious

The first two rules notwithstanding, it has to taste good. Otherwise I'll just resort to a three-course day of chocolate. Then my fingers will grow too large for the emeralds (see Be Spartan, above), which will require resizing and, well, you can see where that's heading.

Use Storage

The Boy Scout motto is, "Be Prepared." Though never sworn in officially, I think it's a good philosophy to live by. Over the years we have tried to accumulate an entire year's supply of food so that if financial or natural disaster strikes, we will, at least, not starve. But what good is food storage if you don't use it? Our menu plan also had to incorporate and rotate this storage so tha:

6. It didn't spoil

7. We could actually survive by eating it

Following all four rules simultaneously was harder than I anticipated. It actually took me a number of years to come up with a plan that worked. Finally, I have it down to a science. Here it is. (If you're math challenged, just trust me. The numbers work. I promise.)

Weekly Menus

Breakfast

Write down one week of breakfast menus that fit your family and schedule.

Lunch

Write down one week of lunch menus that fit your family and schedule.

Dinner

Create five weeks of dinner menus, on a calendar-like grid, according to the following guidelines:

- 12 of the 35 entrées must use only **those** items you can store, long-term, in your cold storage room.

- Remaining 23 entrées can be of any kind you choose

- Add a side dish for each day. Side dishes are the same each week (i.e. Mondays always feature broccoli and fruit salad, Sundays always feature peas and tossed salad, regardless of the entrée choice)

Shopping and Storing

Gather your 12, food storage only recipes and make a shopping list of **all** the items needed. Multiply each item on the list by 30. Purchase all those items and put them in your long-term storage area. (This is an investment and may need to be done over a few months.)

Each weekly shopping trip will include **all** the items needed for the week's menus, both the storage and non-storage meals. The newly purchased food storage items will go **behind** the older ones in your storage system.

When you cook use the oldest foods first with a FIFO (first-in first-out) storage system.

If an emergency strikes and you cannot shop regularly, start rotating only the12, food storage menus. You will have enough food to prepare dinner for an entire year without shopping for more supplies

Using the 12 food storage menus mixed in with the 23 regular menus—as per your menu chart—will allow you to completely rotate your food storage once every three years.

Magic!

System #5: Laundry

Laundry used to be the bane of my existence. And laundry rooms did not make it easier. I've been through them all. Here is a rundown of my past laundry rooms:

- **Nonexistent, requiring the use of a laundromat**: Very romantic for newlyweds for the first three of four times, then drudgery and missing socks.

- **Apartment complex coin laundry**: inconvenient, but not too bad unless it bugs you to have other people touch your underwear.

- **Stacked washer/dryer in mini-bathroom**: An improvement, but no place to fold clean linens (on the toilet seat, maybe?) and always hampered (no pun intended) by the bi-fold door that didn't fully extend.

- **Garage hookups**: What genius concocted this plan to save square footage during construction? Garages are not clean. Garages in South Florida require removal of moderately damp items within 17 minutes of cycle completion to prevent mildew.

- **A proper in-home laundry room, sized eight feet by four feet**: Great...unless you want to go into the room along with the appliances.

These sad excuses for laundry processing resulted in "laundry day" expanding to two or three days. The laundry was spread all over the house. Sorted in the kitchen, folded in the family room, and stacked on the dining room table. It was chaos for those two or three days and all I could do was pray that no one would drop by to see us. If the doorbell rang, the kids were trained to duck silently behind the couch, where we pretended not to be home until the intruders gave up and went away.

Even in gorgeous, luxury homes available for toured viewing, I could only faintly point toward each laundry room and cry, "A man designed this room!" While that comment might be sexist in more than one regard, it is always apparent that someone who never did a stitch of laundry was responsible.

When we built our new, all-custom dream home in 2003, I set out to teach the world of contractors how to design a workable laundry room. When we built our second all-custom dream home in 2010, I refined it. I succeeded. It is gorgeous.

My new laundry room is a large room in the basement. This allows me to shut the door and walk away. I never have to look at it unless I want to and I no longer fear spraining my ankle on a wayward pile of darks in between loads.

Twice per week, an assigned child gathers the laundry and dumps it into a professional grade laundry cart I purchased from a laundry supply outlet. (Admit it. You didn't know such retail places existed, did you?)

Each morning I pop into the laundry room to distribute any new items into the sorting station. This station consists of open shelving that holds six large laundry baskets, one for each of the types of load I clean (darks, lights, dark delicates, light delicates, whites, cleaning cloths). I sort each item appropriately—spraying on stain remover or soaking in the dedicated sink (with integrated washboard) as needed. I also clip off any stray thread or make quick repairs.

Next we come to my pride and joy: the high capacity, high efficiency washer/dryer combo. Rather than the usual washer that holds about two pairs of jeans and one bra (assuming you would, in fact, wash jeans and bras together) and the dryer that takes about three, 60-minute cycles to dry a towel, this miracle washer holds 22 bath towels (I would not joke about this) and the drier dries as fast as the washer washes. This is probably the single most important time-saver invented in the course of my lifetime.

With this amazing system, you must simply look over your dirty, sorted laundry to locate a basket that is absolutely crammed full, over-flowing with filthy, smelly articles of clothing. Then you carefully stuff the washer—using your foot, if necessary—with as many items as possible. Fill the soap, bleach, and softener, push the button, and walk away.

Later, when you really feel like it, walk back in and transfer the clean clothes to the dryer.

Sometime later, when you're in the mood, saunter back in and re-move the fluffy, mountain-fresh load into an empty basket. This goes to the delivery station designed for clean clothes. My delivery station has eight baskets in open shelving, one for each person in the family. Toss each item into the appropriate basket or, if needed, place on a hanger and hang on the rod by the ironing board.

These baskets will remain in place until your children discover their nakedness and run to the basement to retrieve, fold, and put away their own laundry.

The biggest problem you will have with this system is the temp-tation to deceive. Your laundry room will be organized, beautiful, and inviting. The process will require very little time. You will be overcome with an irresistible desire to retreat to the laundry room just to enjoy the ambiance—even when you have no laundry to do. Store some chocolates there, just in case.

The assembly line: an industrial era marvel at work.

System #6: Schoolwork

Homeschooling requires lots and lots of things. Organizing the homeschooling supplies can make learning easier and more fun. Start with these ideas:

Homeschool Room

In the past three houses we've lived in, we have designed a dedicated homeschool room. We don't always use if for all our studies—we aren't bound by it—but it gives us a place to store things and a home base for our work.

Supplies

Homeschool supplies (pencils, paper, rulers, compasses) are all organized just as we organized the other "long-term possessions" above. Have an easily accessible place for everything.

Reference and Research

Since this is our main study room, we fill it with as many of things our kids might need as possible. Here we have dictionaries, atlases, maps, a globe, manipulatives, calculators, microscopes, computers, printers, etc.

Personal Landing Pad

Each child also has a shelf for his or her own work. They have a binder for each subject and keep those, along with any textbooks or workbooks they are using, on their own shelves.

Long-term Storage

We also have an area, up high—out of prime storage space—to put texts and materials that we need, but that no one is currently using.

Study Plan

I've already admitted to inexplicably odd behavior when I'm pregnant. Preferably, I can blame it on the 16% brain shrinkage known to occur during this fragile time. But sometimes life and pregnancy are just too much to cope with simultaneously.

While pregnant with my fifth child everything became overwhelming. Perhaps it was that I had been told he would be a boy and, having four girls, I felt utterly incompetent to mother a child with testosterone—plus that other stuff they come with. Perhaps it was that my eldest was just about to leap, officially, into teenagerhood, and I was terrified at the ramifications.

Whatever the cause(s), my concerns about parenting and homeschooling all these children at once reached a frenzied peak that prevented me from sleeping or functioning rationally. (Unfortunately, it did not curb my craving for chocolate or sweet and sour cabbage.)

As is my nature, I attempted to regain a feeling of control over my life by organizing excessively.

First, I organized all the spices alphabetically. Then I gathered all the ideas I had collected over the years that would create our ideal pre-K through 12 genius education curricula. After hours and hours of pouring over them further, I molded them into a cohesive program.

The next step is one I hesitate to mention. It's not one I recommend to you. I first revealed it when speaking at a UHEA convention out of a deep inner need to reveal that I'm easily as weird as anyone else. (They were duly convinced.) Again, I'm not suggesting that you do this; I just want to disclose what made me feel better about homeschooling in a situation of mental stress.

Once everything was outlined, I created a Gantt chart for each child on the computer. Each item was designed so that, over time, the color changed to show the percentage completed. Now I have a complete visual timeline of what every single child has done and what he or she has yet to do before reaching adulthood.

Next, I used the Gantt charts to create daily schedules. These began as a scroll of paper, sticky tack, and slips of colored cardstock. This included a daily calendar, with rows for time slots, and color-coded columns for each person. First, all the "hard" times were filled in: music lessons, church, athletic classes, and club meetings. Then academic work, chores, meals, family devotional, etc. were scheduled around them in a reasonable fashion.

After a few days of rearranging, I had a beautiful, rainbow-colored schedule to carry me through the first year of my new baby's life. To someone who craves order, this helped me relax enough to think and get ready for the birth.

While this is more structured than I would normally choose, having a large family with a wide age range can be a challenge. Incorporating our long-term goals into a workable schedule helped me to see that it really was doable. It gave me a framework to serve as the basis for our days. I could relax, knowing I wouldn't neglect significant subjects.

Over time this scroll morphed into a colorful computer spreadsheet that we used for well over a decade. Now, we simply calendar block each child's assignments on a shared calendar app, with one item for each subject and any necessary details.

We rework the schedule about three times each year (usually September, January, and May). In the 20 years since creating them, we've never followed the schedules to the letter, but they've allowed us to accomplish a lot, with a lot of people, without undue aggravation.

The point isn't for you to obsess, but rather for you to find a method that will allow you to feel comfortably in charge of your life and the direction your family is heading. And remember, when you find the method, you aren't obligated to tell anyone about it. There's always someone weirder than you.

Final Thoughts

For some of you, getting **everything** in your lives will be an easy tweak. Perhaps everything is already in order. Adding in a homeschool system may be the only change.

For others, organizing everything will be overwhelming. Please don't let this be a roadblock! Like everything else in this process, you can take baby steps toward organizing and prioritizing your home and life. One day and step at a time.

Make sure, as you work through each system, you personalize it to fit your family. There is a system that will work for you, but it will be yours alone. Find that sweet spot and it will be fairly simple to stick to it.

For resources and downloads relating to Habit #3, go to:
https://the7successhabitsofhomeschoolers.com/habit3

Habit 4: Everybody Wins

Michael, if you can't pass, you can't play.

Coach Dean Smith (to Michael Jordan in his freshman year at UNC)

This is my favorite step to talk about, and yet the most difficult for me to implement. No matter how long I homeschool, there seems to be entrenched in the back of my mind the fundamental rule that the school district (which would be me) sets the curricular requirements and the teacher (who would also be me) sets the agenda—and the student joyfully follows along without any choice in the matter and without any input.

While this may be the most efficient way to run a district with a billion kids (and even more administrators), it's not the most effective way to homeschool. Neither is it the most fun.

Homeschooling allows families to be in charge. Your kids win and you win! If you can move out of the mindset that says the authority figure is the sole dictator, you can create an environment in which both parents and children will love not only the process of education, but the outcome as well. It's not one-sided (or even two-sided). **Everybody wins**.

Having the crucial, general, long-term goals discussed in Step 2 does not lock you into specific, inflexible, short-term methods. It opens up endless possibilities. You can reach the goals you have carefully determined are essential to a high-quality adult life—and you can do it in a way your children will love!

Textbooks

I remember like it was yesterday. I had to stay in from recess in sixth grade. Instead of doing my social studies assignment, I had spent the hour goofing off. Missing recess was my penance.

Generally, I was a good student (although I "visited with my neighbor too much"), but this particular class just made my head throb. As punishment, I sat for the entire 45 minutes (remember when recess was that long in the olden days?), reading and rereading the same paragraph in the dreaded maize-colored textbook. I hated the color. I hated the content. And I just could not keep focused for even one paragraph as it droned on and on. It was probably the singular most boring moment of my life and probably the only time I was seriously tempted to pull the fire alarm. I even began fantasizing about more interesting things like washing dishes and cleaning baseboards.

Suffice it to say, if you hate textbooks, I feel your pain. Just because a publisher is willing to put something on the market, does not make it worthy of the time it takes to read. If you child is suffering through a text, hoping you'll suddenly remember the garage needs to be cleaned, there is probably a reason. Consider the possibility that the text is a dud, no matter how highly recommended by other homeschool moms.

But please believe me when I say there really are some great textbooks out there, too. You just have to dig a bit. This old standby really can be the best way to learn some subjects, particularly those that require some kind of sequential learning. Don't disregard this choice just because you have a bad, maize-colored textbook memory.

If you're using a particular textbook to teach a subject, and it isn't interesting or exciting, one option is to find a new one! Ask for recommendations, from both parents and other kids. You may find a perfect fit.

Textbook Outlines

You can also use a textbook as a course outline. Rather than following the text itself, just use the table of contents of a sound, comprehensive text to give a framework to design your own study of the same topic. It gives you a head start on the structure, while allowing the actual content to be personalized to your family with the most interesting resources you can find.

Unit Studies

A unit study is an in-depth learning experience based on a particular topic. Generally, a unit study incorporates many subjects, such as history, art, geography, science, etc., all into the same topical study.

Any topic of interest can be used. Allowing your children to choose subjects they love, such as baseball, horses, flowers, or ancient Greece, makes learning interesting and exciting to them. In past years we've studied gardening, royalty, the solar system, machines, and all sorts of other things in this way.

After a few years of experimenting, we ended up using studies mostly for elementary and middle school social studies. We've studied ancient Egypt, Middle Ages, and ancient Greece, and the Renaissance and Reformation.

When I first wrote this book and had younger kids, we were studying American pioneers and the trek west. In that unit we read first-hand biographical accounts (we particularly enjoyed them when the writer was an ancestor!), drew pictures of the stories, watched movies depicting the time period, mapped out the travel route, cooked pioneer food, played pioneer games, and did pioneer crafts. To end the unit, we visited a historic site that is a re-creation of a pioneer village.

As teens, each of my children went on a three-day "pioneer trek" with my husband and a large group of other teens. They dressed in pioneer clothing, marched miles and miles each day pulling a handcart, and slept under the stars—all in Wyoming, where some of the pioneers actually crossed the plains. Having the past intense historical study enhanced these trips, since they had some real examples and knowledge.

This kind of study requires some advanced preparation, but it's well worth it. Kids usually look forward to them. Do you really imagine they would learn more sitting in a classroom listening to a lecture? Me neither.

Online Courses

In 1994 I created my first website. It was a hand-coded homeschool curriculum catalog for my company, Bright Spark Press. Since those early days of websites, the number of online offerings has exploded.

Quality content available on the internet is abundant. Static information as well as interactive sites and apps cover every content area. As usual, some are dry, buggy, and/or inaccurate. Some are very high quality. Spend some time to weed through the options.

Many universities and public high schools offer online courses and grant credit after completion. Some are entirely free!

Co-op Groups

When a number of families get together to share some of their learning, it's called a co-op (or cooperative) group.

There are limitless ways to organize group learning and some homeschoolers depend on the support, diversity, and relationships that are fostered in such groups. Find some like-minded folks and decide what things you'd like to learn together.

You can meet once per month to discuss a book you've read at home. You can meet every other week for life skills or activities. Some groups meet once per week for sports or performance rehearsals. You can meet two or three times per week for more intense classes. Or study any topic under (or above!) the sun and do it with the size and frequency that meets your needs.

One good friend of mine has been involved in a co-op for over a decade. The kids meet every Friday, each mother teaching a different topic. The kids have grown up together, have great fun, and won't miss it.

I have created a number of topic specific homeschool groups over the years. My approach is to find an interest one (or more) of my children has, and invite other homeschoolers to join in a group with that focus. Here are some I have headed up:

- Youth choir

- Girls book group

- Girls activity club

- Recognition day

- Park day

- Teen boys board game club

- Teen swing choir

- Teen activity night

- Teen filmmaker club

If you see an unmet need, fill it and invite others to join!

Community Classes

Most cities offer a wide range of classes at nominal prices through their community education program. Local residents in community centers and schools around the country teach these courses. They can play an important role in your homeschooling and range from cooking to belly dancing to business finance to web design to vegetable gardening.

We have used these programs for dance classes, babysitting courses, aerobics classes, flower arranging, theater, stage lighting design, and ACT prep. Other possibilities are martial arts, sports teams, swimming, arts and crafts, software expertise, investing, college scholarship planning, and more.

Look into community choirs, orchestras, and bands to join, as well as community theater productions, on stage or behind the scenes.

Some of my fondest memories as a child were performing at Valley Center Theatre, getting my first musical lead and recording a soundtrack. I continued to perform in college, and was nominated as the Best Actress in a Musical award for playing Fiona in *Brigadoon*. It wasn't Broadway, but it was a great experience all around.

Local Businesses

Don't neglect all the local businesses that offer courses and services.

Craft stores often give classes in oil painting, scrapbooking, or similar things. Tax preparers often teach clients how to use software or about the latest home business deductions. One art center in our area gives classes in sculpture, stained glass, and even glass blowing.

There are many businesses that focus on physical education. Martial arts and dance studios, gyms that give gymnastics and tumbling training, ice skating and other specialties are available in most areas. One daughter took riding and dressage lessons from a local stable for years. Three of my daughters and I took Irish dance lessons together at a studio that encouraged family participation.

All of my kids (and my husband and I) took karate lessons, two of them reaching black belt status. Our youngest has been taking parkour (or urban gymnastics) for a few years from a local studio and is very passionate about it.

If there is a skill out there, you can find someone to teach it. You can offer to teach it to others as well.

Apprenticeships

Call this the old-fashioned way to learn if you want, but it's still one of the best. If your child wants to learn a trade or skill, what better way to do it than directly from a master?

Those who teach in schools may not be most proficient in their fields. How many truly superb potters teach junior high art class? If your child is yearning to throw gorgeous pots, who better to learn from than a local artisan who makes his living with clay?

Look for a professional and ask if s/he can teach your child. Perhaps your child can even exchange some labor for his lessons.

I have a friend who visited a metal foundry on a Cub Scout field trip. He fell in love with the place and bugged the owner until he let him come by after school to sweep up and do odd jobs. Today, after years of being taught by the master, he owns the company.

Performances & Exhibits

Some things just don't lend themselves to bookwork, but only come experientially.

Go to a play, a concert, or a recital. Attend an exhibit or art show. These can be not only great entertainment, but very educational and motivating.

Recently, local movie theaters have started carrying live satellite feeds of all sorts of performances, including those from the Metropolitan Opera. Look into that possible diversion for an afternoon.

When I was a child, my parents had season tickets to the community symphony every year. The admission was free and the concerts were performed in a beautiful old tabernacle. I had no idea how I would be influenced by these performances, but they helped create a life-long love of music and familiarity with classic culture.

Colleges & Universities

If you live in a college town, count your blessings. Many institutions of higher education add a level of culture and accessibility that is hard to find elsewhere. The prices are usually very reasonable and the quality is often superb. Recitals and other student performances are often free of charge.

My parents took me to see the opera *The Magic Flute* at BYU when I was 2. At that moment I knew I wanted to be a Broadway star. We saw hundreds of plays, musicals, concerts, and recitals as I grew up. It exposed me to so many styles and instruments that music became a passion and a great source of joy in my life.

Be forewarned. Unfortunately, these days you need to be more selective with college fare. When I was young, we saw *The Importance of Being Ernest*, *Bye Bye Birdie*, and *Pippin* at local universities. Since then I've seen colleges host performances that were entirely inappropriate for children—not to mention adults—with high sexual content and loaded with vulgarity. That's not quite the cultural education I'm looking for.

Show Off

When Jessica was in public school kindergarten, her class's artwork was displayed at both McDonald's and the public library. This was a fun form of recognition. Homeschoolers don't always have ready access to display their works, along with a built-in fan base. But you can create one just as schools do.

Local libraries or community centers will often be pleased to show your quality work. Even businesses will sometimes sponsor a contest and display the results. Just ask!

Consider hosting a "Recognition Day" for other homeschoolers once per month. Invite others to bring an assignment, a project, or a performance, and share it with others. In Florida I headed up such an event. We themed the event each month by subject. January might be reserved for science projects, February for language arts, March for visual arts, April for life skills, etc. One month was always open to anything at all.

It was great to allow the children to show their work to their peers, to applaud, and give some well-deserved recognition for a job well done.

Board Games

Games are a fabulous way to add fun to the mix. I'm not talking about drill worksheets disguised as games—which are a dime a dozen and don't fool even a first grader—but well-designed games that either require knowledge and skill or give a strategic advantage for learning new information.

There are a number of companies that have been very successful at creating such quality games. They are well worth the investment. Some of the best are from specialty companies, but even a browse through the local discount store will reveal all sorts of word games, critical thinking games, and others that will keep the brain engaged.

Some of our favorite educational games are:

Acquire	Proof!
Apples to Apples	Pylos
Azul	Quarto
Balderdash	Quiddler
Bananagrams	Quixo
Blokus	Quoridor
Boggle	Qwirkle
Chess	Racko
Clue	Risk
Continent Race	Rumis

Election Night	Rummikub
Genius Marble Run	Rush Hour
Global Pursuit	Scattergories
Gravity Maze	Scrabble
Guess in 10	Sequence
Horse-opoly	Set
Ingenious	Shapes Up
Managing My Allowance	Skyjo
Monopoly	Smath
Muggins & Knockout	Snap Circuits
One Up!	Taboo
Pandemic	Trekking the National Parks
Payday	Where in the World?
Planet	The World Game
Prime Club	Yinsh

Music

Forget fish oil and ginkgo biloba. Music is the real brain booster. Not only is it a wonderful end in itself, music also helps brain development in every subject. In addition, it can serve as a great hook for memorizing just about anything.

When my fourth daughter, Monica, was one year old, I started a homeschool choir for elementary-aged children. Part of our repertoire included a whole slew of educational songs. We learned songs about the geography of U.S. states and capitals, various continents, and mountains around the world. We memorized songs of the bones of the body, the planets in the solar system, inventors, explorers, and the days of the week and months of the year. A favorite song described the entire organization of the three branches of government.

There is downloadable music available to teach math facts, scriptures, and the Preamble to the Constitution. Singing patriotic hymns and pieces from different historical periods is another way to incorporate music.

Because the songs were well-written and engaging, it was easy to memorize the information. And it was a lot of fun. It made our children much more conversant in history, geography, and current events, and it made for a foolproof way to impress the neighborhood homeschooling skeptics.

Even better, eight years later, in the midst of Jessica's freshman year at college, she aced all the geography exams in her world civilization class (knocking the grading curve for a loop), using the songs she had learned in elementary school. Her professor was amazed.

Summer Camps

Admittedly, some camps are nothing more than the summer version of day care, and the kids not better behaved than zoo animals. Been there; done that. But if you look hard, you might find some high-quality experiences.

When I was a teen, I attended a symphony orchestra camp and, later, a two-week theater workshop. They were highlights that impacted me for years.

For the past 19 years my children have attended camps at the same local university and they are still superb. The primary teachers were not high school or college kids who were otherwise unemployed—they were the professors and coaches and experts in the field in question. The best of the best.

To date, my kids have attended the following camps:

- 7 Habits for youth

- Ballroom dance

- Basketball

- Cheerleading

- Dance medley

- Diving

- Folk dance

- Musical dance theater

- Multi-sport camp

- Outdoor adventure sports

- Pioneer trek

- Soccer

- Youth leadership and spirituality

We plan on using these camps every year, as they have been so enjoyable and educational. The kids look forward to this experience and save their money all year long to attend.

In addition to professionally designed camps, sometimes we've created our own. One summer, for example, Samson and Caleb (then seven- and three-years old respectively) wanted two camps that weren't available to them, due to their ages. My husband created daylong bowling and golf camps for them. The boys invited 10-year-old Monica to join. They turned out to be the hits of the summer.

Public & Private Schools

Yes, I said it. School.

When my children begin ninth grade, they begin participating in a daily religion course. Because it is geared toward students who are in public schools, it allows students to get released-time from regular classes for one period. The buildings used are generally located next to public schools and follow the school's schedule.

When they begin these courses—which continue through 12th grade—our family must provide transportation as well as accommodate the public-school schedule. Since they are already near the school, we encourage them to look for a school class or two they will enjoy. The choice is left to them, but usually they have been able to find something that contributed to their education.

To date they have taken: musical theater, drama, dance, madrigals, show choir, debate, ceramics, welding, art, drafting, debate, child development (including a full-scale child care facility), peer advisory council, etc. These have all been enjoyable and they have opened up other school opportunities, such as performing in musical productions and competing in tournaments.

My oldest four children have had the opportunity to play lead roles and had solos in school performances. Jessica was chosen as one of the three top drama students at the high school. Alana won best actor at state Shakespeare competition for the title role in *Titus Andronicus* (yes, playing a male role) along with a full college scholarship.

Not all experiences were positive. One daughter tried out an English class. There she learned that she already knew far more than most kids her age in that subject.

"Conjunctions! I'm in 9th grade and we spent two weeks on conjunctions!"

She chose to drop that class after the first term. I count that as a positive learning experience, too!

If your local school has a great drama program, an award-winning choir, a fabulous chemistry teacher (as opposed to a cheerleading coach who is posing as a science instructor), a superb horticulture program, or a dual-enrollment option that provides college credit, then use them. (You already paid the tuition.)

Taking advantage of the very best that schools have to offer—and leaving the rest—has given my children some astounding memories and enhanced their educations.

With so many options available, it's easy to adjust homeschooling to fit both the child and the parent. And when you do, everybody wins.

Final Thoughts

The best homeschooling isn't "my way or the highway" with the parents as traffic cop. Nor does it have to be free-roaming kids doing whatever seems the most compelling at a given moment in time.

Instead, take the extra time and effort to make sure everybody wins. How can you reach those ends that are crucial while making it the most interesting, compelling, exciting, fun experience it can be? Parents don't need to entertain their children or jump through hoops, but it's not difficult to make adjustments that motivate children to engage in their own learning. Each child is unique and you now have the perfect opportunity to make education personal.

For resources and downloads relating to Habit #4, go to:
https://the7successhabitsofhomeschoolers.com/habit4

Habit 5: It's All About Time

*To every thing there is a season, and a time to every pur-
pose under the heaven: A time to be born, and a time to
die; a time to plant, and a time to pluck up that which is
planted; A time to kill, and a time to heal; a time to break
down, and a time to build up; A time to weep, and a time
to laugh; a time to mourn, and a time to dance.*

Ecclesiastes 3: 1–4

One of the greatest blessings of homeschooling is time. Time to go
sledding on the first snow day of the season. Time to stay up late
to watch a meteor shower. Time to marvel at kittens being born. Time
to mourn the death of a grandparent. Time to lie in the sun on the first
warm day of spring.

A few years ago, a dear friend died cancer in his thirties. He left a
widow and three young children. In no time they were back in school,
in an attempt to keep a sense of normalcy and to prevent the additional

stress of getting behind. Undoubtedly it was the right choice for this wonderful family, but I was struck by how the schools and schedules were allowed to dictate even how the children mourned the loss of their father.

As homeschoolers, we have an incredible gift in largely being able to choose a schedule that suits our family. You will have the time to deeply know and understand each child. They will still surprise you regularly, but you probably won't be blindsided by their behavior. (Your mileage may vary!)

Homeschoolers not only choose the path to follow, they choose the speed as well. The freedom provides many opportunities for bonding.

Vacation & Recreation

Florida summers are no fun, with 98-degree temperatures in 98% humidity. But the winters are gorgeous! So, when we lived there, we did more summer bookwork (when being outside was miserable) and took more vacations in the winter—when it was gorgeous outside, and everyone else was stuck in school. What a bonus to go to Disneyworld in February, when the weather was wondrous and the lines were minimal!

When my husband was a professor at a university, his academic calendar was utterly unrelated to that of the local primary schools. Lucky for us. When he had time off—and all the neighborhood children were in school—we went to the beach, the park, the children's museum, and had quality family time without the crowds everyone else faced.

Rather than take school days off for "teacher development days" and the NEA convention, we celebrate Christmas all December long decorating, baking, making gifts, and singing. There are so many amazing family events to attend and far too many cookies to eat to worry about regular schoolwork (or finals) all month.

Kid Dates & Kid Trips

Each week my husband has a "date" alone with one of our children. Over the years he rotated through the six of them (and later, those who were still living at home), giving each one a chance to choose something fun to do just with Dad. As homeschoolers, we have the flexibility to do this any day or time, whenever it best suits the situation.

Each new teenager also looked forward to going with Sam on one of his business trips. They spent lots of time together and stayed an extra day or two to see the sites of the city. These always occurred smack dab in the middle of the school year—when crowds were minimal. Jessica wend to Philadelphia, Belinda to Dallas, and Alana to Boston. Monica, Samson, and Caleb all chose to go to different areas of Florida.

One on One

More than mere scheduling, homeschooling gives you a chance to know and understand each one of your children.

If my teenage girls had to be on the bus at 6:52 am like their peers, we would have missed hours and hours and hours of late-night discussions. These conversations were amazing. They weren't **always** fun and they weren't **always** pleasant, but the sheer volume of time spent and the vast array of topics covered defined our relationships. And they happened when the girls needed them—which somehow very often happened to be after midnight—without the consequence of ruining the whole next day.

Sometimes I hear stories about large homeschooling families that never have family problems. Apparently, they do needlework in the parlor while engaging in refined conversation all day long. They always get along famously and lovingly and are best friends. And they never seem to have that growing need for autonomy that sometimes brings conflict.

I want to be clear; my family is entirely "normal" in this regard. For better or worse, sometimes the togetherness is more than they want and even my sage advice is not always correct or welcome. Still, they were able to be involved in each other's lives.

When one of my college daughters—the one who couldn't stand me just two short years earlier—sent a card saying I was her "best friend," called every day to ask for advice or just to chat, and texted me late at night just to say, "I love you. I miss you." it was more than full payback for all the sleep deprivation.

I am so very blessed to have been with my children when they needed me. Whenever that happened to be.

When you are actually with your kids, you've got a head start into their hearts. Quality time requires quantity time. Homeschooling has the extraordinary benefit of giving you 15,000 more hours with each of your children than if they were in school. What a blessing, to get your children back!

Final Thoughts

Like many other things you are accustomed to from public schooling, rigid school schedules—dictated by a bunch of "stakeholders" you've never met—are unnecessary and often problematic. Your children absolutely do not need 180 days of seven "seat time" hours per year to become educated, intelligent, productive adults. I promise they do not.

Consider your children and your family (and everything else applicable) when determining your homeschool schedule.

You have so much more control over your time now! It's an opportunity to do more than you ever imagined. Take full advantage of it!

For resources and downloads relating to Habit #5, go to:
https://the7successhabitsofhomeschoolers.com/habit5

Habit 6: Synergize
$1+1=3^2$

> *Teamwork is the ability to work together toward a common vision. The ability to direct individual accomplishments toward organizational objectives. It is the fuel that allows common people to attain uncommon results.*

Andrew Carnegie

Synergy is described as when cooperation results in a product that is greater than the sum of its parts. Stephen Covey's version of synergy is $1 + 1 = 3$. But education is transformational in every part of life. So, the synergy is $1 + 1 = 3^2$, because when you apply synergy to education, the benefit is exponential!

You are in charge. You have the power. You can make homeschool the best possible experience.

One day I realized I was benefiting from homeschooling as much as my kids. I love it and don't ever want to stop. That being the case, one of my goals is to make homeschooling as attractive to my children as possible.

Applying synergy is the key to keeping out of a rut. If things seem a little blasé or predictable, do something different. Work with your kids and their interests to shake things up. Make homeschool fun and exciting!

Field Trips

Schools have occasional field trips for a reason, and they really are onto something. Day trips to new and interesting locations build excitement, give a diversion from the typical schedule, and remove the mundane—no matter what education method you follow. If things begin to get a little bogged down, get out and do something different.

Field trips are easy to set up. You can go just about anywhere you can imagine and most places that welcome public school children will accommodate homeschool groups as well. You can see the behind-the-scenes views that aren't generally available to the public. Call ahead and invite some friends and you can usually get a school discount as well.

But the best thing about homeschool field trips is that they can be personalized to fit the interests of your children and the particular things they are studying. They can expose them to amazing new things and encourage them in areas they might not otherwise pursue. You can design the best field trips to augment their studies.

Below are some great places to consider:

- Airport

- Amusement park

- Animal watching

- Aquariums

- Archaeological sites

- Art institute, museum, or exhibit

- Asphalt plant

- Athletic event, academy, or stadium

- Auto assembly line

- Aviary

- Bakery

- Bank

- Beach

- Beekeeper

- Bread factory

- Boat, ferry, or glass-bottomed boat ride

- Builder supply store

- Butcher shop

- Camping

- Candy shop or factory

- Ceramic shop

- Christmas tree farm

- Computer company

- Concert or recital

- Construction site

- County circuit court

- Dairy

- Dance concert or performance

- Donut shop

- Dry cleaner

- Ethnic museum or festival

- Fabric shop

- Farm, plain or organic

- Fair, state or county

- Festival

- Fire station

- Fish hatchery or fishing

- Foundry

- Government offices

- Gravel pit

- Grocery store

- Harbor authority tour

- Hiking

- Historic festival

- Historic sites

- Holiday festivities

- Hunting

- Industrial plant

- Instrument craftsman

- Landfill

- Landmarks

- Library tour

- Magistrate court

- Mall security

- Mattress factory

- Mines

- Musical concert or performance

- Museum

- National monument

- Nature reserve

- Newspaper publisher

- Nuclear reactor

- Nursery

- Oceanographic center or museum

- Orchard, grove, or vineyard

- Park

- Photo developer

- Picnic

- Police or mounted police station

- Post office

- Power plant

- Prison or jail

- Public or private school

- Race track

- Radio station

- Recycling center

- Religious building or ceremony

- Resort conference center

- Restaurants

- Road crew

- Rock or gem quarry

- Science museum or exhibit

- Sewage and water treatment plant

- Shipyard

- Shoe repair shop

- Space center or museum

- State capitol

- Steel mill

- Television station

- Theater production or tour

- Theme park

- Train, tram, or trolley ride

- University science laboratory

- Walks

- Zoo or animal preserve

We've used dozens of these ideas and it's always been a great addition to our other schooling.

Libraries

Nothing fosters a love of independent learning better than a leisurely afternoon at a great public library. If you are blessed to have one within a reasonable distance, take advantage of it often.

My favorite libraries are those that allow children the privilege of having their very own library cards and impose no book limit. Piling into the van with laundry baskets soon-to-be filled with adventures of every kind is a special kind of thrill.

Let your kids loose to gather to their hearts' content. You won't have to persuade them to read when you get home. My kids were typically immersed in reading the minute we got into the car to go home.

You will have to pay fines for overdue books. Just make it part of your budget like food and toilet paper. It's inevitable.

Service Projects

There is no better cure, I'm convinced, for the typical self-centeredness and hypersensitivity of tweens and teens than a good dose of looking away from the mirror and the social scene. Homeschooling give you the time and flexibility to build major acts of goodness right into their curriculum.

Perhaps you can find a service that correlates to their studies. You might find something in an area that is very interesting to your child. Maybe you're looking for something to do as an entire family. One year I started a homeschool service club, combining service with socialization. In whatever way works best for your family, make the time to do good for others. You'll actually do the most good for your own family.

Clubs

Contrary to popular belief, homeschooled children are no more likely to be anti-social freaks than the rest of the neighbor kids. And they love getting together with those with similar interests just like anyone. Joining a club is a great way to accommodate the desire for peer interaction in a good environment.

If you can't find one in your area or from your support group, create it yourself. It's easy. Look for things your child likes to do and invite others to do it at a regular place and time. Now you officially have a club.

When Jessica was ten, she wanted more time to play with friends. Most of the kids her age in our neighborhood were not only gone all day, but involved in before- and after-school care as well, since both of their parents worked. We discussed our options and decided to start the Girls Club.

Belinda was seven, so I designed the club for girls age seven to ten. (Always try to get the biggest bang for your buck.) The girls thought once per month would be enough. Each club member would take a turn planning, hosting, and providing refreshments.

Once we settled on the format, I sent an email to local homeschoolers inviting them. The response was overwhelming. We ended up with well over 20 girls in the club, and that little group spawned two other clubs for girls and a couple more for boys. They did all sorts of fun things, from craft hours, to sports adventures, to park days, to dress-up tea parties with their dolls. The girls made friends and had a lot of fun.

Later Monica was in a club called Liberty Ladies with a bunch of her peers and it was a favorite activity she anticipated twice per month.

A few years ago, with three teenage daughters in the house, we got together with some other parents of teens and planned a new club, Teen Scene. This group also meets once per month, but they meet on a weekend evening and their events are generally much bigger and bolder. They play laser tag, have elaborate Halloween parties, go rock climbing, ice blocking, and have pizza parties. You know, teen stuff. Every year we host the big spring barbecue bash.

Once we even had a local recording artist agree to give a free concert for the kids in exchange for offering some of her CDs for sale afterward. It was a great show, the artist was very personable, and she spent time answering all the questions the kids had about performing, recording, and writing music.

Teen Scene was a great success with up to 70 kids attending the biggest of the events each year. And, to be honest, I'd never have 70 non-homeschooled teens at my house at once!

A couple of years ago—this time with two teenage sons—we planned a boys' game club. Kids came every week for a couple of hours to play board games, eat snacks, and socialize.

Currently we host a filmmaker club for high school age guys and gals. For two hours every week, the members meet up at our house. In that time, they brainstorm, script, and film a video. During the week to follow, Caleb (who also serves as the videographer), edits the film and puts it up on his YouTube channel, BroAntics.

Other fun club ideas focus on chess, crochet, dance, karate, sports, and woodcarving. You can create a club around any hobby or activity. The sky's the limit.

Kick-off Events

In the 90s, the kids chose to spend a year studying ancient Egypt. We had so many resources and so many things to learn and do that one year turned to two and then almost three. The kids were having a great time building pyramids out of blocks, recreating a pharaoh's nemes crown, and learning the proper placement of entrails during mummification but, honestly, I just couldn't stand it any more!

I had tried for some months to hurry along the unit to a reasonable conclusion, but the kids kept finding one more thing they wanted to do, really important things like making papier mâché replicas of King Tut's death mask and clay models of the topography of Egypt. My efforts to move on were in vain.

Then I saw an advertisement in the newspaper. The Society for Creative Anachronism (SCA) was coming to town, and they were putting on a fabulous Renaissance Festival in the neighboring city of Fort Lauderdale.

"Wow! Look at this! Knights and maidens and gypsies and costumes and jousting and food and games. Look at all these cool things. Darn! If only we were studying Renaissance & Reformation now!"

Bright children see the value in new experiences. It only took us three weeks to become utterly disenchanted with Egypt, which, coincidentally, aligned almost to the minute with SCA's grand entrance into town.

The Renaissance Festival became the exciting first day of the study of a new historic era. It was also the day I realized that having an exciting event to kick-off a unit was a great thing to anticipate. It builds enthusiasm and adds excitement. And it's just plain fun.

Ending Events

The same can be said of planning a fun event to mark the end of a study. Let the excitement build as you prepare to do a big send-off with a party, special event, or other adventure.

We culminated one series of activities with a Cinco de Mayo party, inviting friends and neighbors. This is still a fun memory, especially for Belinda who offered her handmade piñata as the sweet finale.

Home Business

I graduated from college three weeks after my first daughter was born. My husband, however, took four more years to finish all his graduate degrees while working as a research assistant. By the time he had morphed into Dr. Smith and was ready to step into his first full-time job, we had two children. (You can read that, "dirt poor.")

Since I desperately wanted to stay home with my children, but also had a desire to eat, I opened my first home business that same year. Long after the financial need was gone, this has remained a passion for me. I love business and making money. It's a rewarding challenge. But running a business takes time and can get in the way of educating your children.

What's a homeschooler to do? Involve them!

Running a business can provide one of the best hands-on education opportunities around. Give your children any job they can handle. Teach them the skills you use in your business. Educate them about the structure and the finances. Pay them as the learn.

Your work time can double as family time and your children will get an amazing boost toward life as an entrepreneur.

A friend who is a brilliant entrepreneur took this to the next step by helping her children create businesses of their own. One summer, her oldest son—an expert swimmer trained in lifesaving—offered his services as a lifeguard at his own backyard pool. The neighbor children were invited to swim, for a fee, during particular hours while he provided safety.

Her oldest daughter bought a professional-looking vendor stand and sold all sorts of snacks and treats to the swimmers. The neighbor kids and parents loved the service. My friend's kids made some good money, had fun, and learned a lot about budgeting, business expenses, and advertising while providing valued services and products to their neighbors.

Game Day

You can schedule your days in endless ways. Instead of being a slave to your schedule, make the schedule work for you.

We love games and have a ton of them, but found we rarely played them. Many are extremely educational, but we just didn't make the time.

For a number of years, we structured our schoolwork so that Monday and Friday were our heaviest academic days. Tuesday and Thursday were moderate days and the days they attended sports and dance classes. Wednesday—right smack dab in the middle of the week—started with a brief bit of schoolwork and then it was nothing but fun and games until late afternoon.

What better way to get over "hump day" than to break up the week with a fun diversion?

Every Wednesday, we set aside the books and pulled out the fun. We all looked forward to the break in a busy week and it gave us some downtime together.

Your Expertise

What do you do well? What are your skills? Offer them to local homeschoolers and create an atmosphere of sharing and mutual benefit.

Singing is one of my favorite things in life. I'd rather sing for an audience than almost anything in the world. When some of my children began expressing the desire for performing opportunities—and I spent a few months chauffeuring them to another city to participate—it occurred to me that I could provide the same thing in my own home.

My first choir was for elementary-aged kids, including three of my own. Another mom was the accompanist and we sang all sorts of fun, traditional, patriotic, and educational songs. We had a great time together, learned valuable performing skills, and made great friends.

Years later, in a different state, I started a swing choir for teen girls, since I had three. I held auditions, chose costumes, and selected music. Within a few months, SwingShift Singers was off and running. This small, female, audition-only swing choir gave my own children and many others the opportunity to sing and dance and perform (in sequins!)—without having to go to public school. We continued with that choir for nearly three years until we were ready to try something new.

Another time I offered a class in stage dialects to budding thespians. It was only one semester long—so no long-term commitment was required—but it was still fun and educational.

Others in my area have offered classes in sewing, cooking, bicycle repair, needlework, biology, math games, art, short story writing, drama, small engine repair, ballroom dance, solar power, wood working, etc.

If you know it, share it! And encourage others to do the same. The whole homeschooling community benefits from cooperative efforts.

Connections

When we moved to Utah, we struggled to find a martial arts school that used the same method we had studied in Florida. After some time researching and visiting different groups, we found a relatively new school that taught Ed Parker Kenpo Karate. It was just what we were looking for.

During our tenure there, the school expanded to include karate, gymnastics, and dance. Two years later, I had three children studying karate and participating on the karate demo team. One wanted to add gymnastics to her athletic endeavors, another wanted to try dance, and my oldest son had just become old enough to join the karate classes—and he couldn't wait to jump, kick, and chop with his sisters.

I refused. I simply could not add any more drive-and-wait time to my crowded schedule. I was swamped. But as the pleas persisted, I began to ponder what I could do to accommodate these desires without breaking my emotional bank.

The sports academy they attended was a business. The goal of the business is to make money by providing a quality athletic experience to children and adults. I'm a homeschooler, and my job is to provide a quality educational experience to my children. If both needs can be met simultaneously, we'll have an arms-length transaction—something that will benefit all involved.

After some thought I came up with a plan I felt would serve both parties. I wrote up my ideas and presented them to the owner of the studio.

In a nutshell, my proposal was this: You have a great facility, but it sits empty all day long, waiting for your students to get out of school. You have a great, untapped market in homeschoolers who want a quality athletic experience and are not tied to a schedule during the day. You only need to cover the costs of additional instructors and some extra administration in order to break even. The other facility expenses are sunk costs.

Here were the parameters. This market (homeschoolers) has lim-ited free time (having taken on additional responsibilities) and limited income (almost all are single-income families). If you can provide a program that allows homeschooling parents to come to the facility one time, to give all their children a quality experience—at a great price—I can fill your facility.

After a number of months of discussion and planning, the owner created a wonderful two-hour sports rotation program: three age groups, three athletic events, and a bargain price. Within a few weeks, enough of the classes were at capacity that it warranted a new track to fill the demand.

Look at the things you already do and the connections you have in the community. There are myriad ways to create world-class opportunities for homeschoolers in your area if you tap into that market.

Scheduled Downtime

We school year-round. This has so many advantages. It prevents learning gaps caused by long absences from academic work. It allows us to take many days off during the year—when the mood strikes us, when it fits our schedule, or when some great event comes up. It gives us structure and stability no matter what the season. We never have to worry about "how to entertain the kids all summer" or "how to adjust to the new school year" because it's an ongoing endeavor that never ends.

With a few exceptions—like holidays, birthdays, and family vacations—for the first number of years, school was a fixed part of the everyday plan.

One year, a couple of my kids were envious of the neighborhood kids who were going to get a day off school for teacher training. I was surprised. Reminding them that they had already had more days off than any of their peers didn't change their perception.

Finally, I realized that when you only have downtime when it spontaneously occurs, you miss the excitement and anticipation that comes when you have a vacation day planned far in advance. Even if your children really enjoy their schooling, everyone loves a day of complete, utter freedom. And looking forward to it is part of the pleasure.

Schedule some specific vacation time and let your kids plan on it.

Final Thoughts

Forget the obligatory events or procedures your local school engages in every year. What is most meaningful to **your children**? What do they want to do or see? Where can they go that fits perfectly with their studies and interests? What will be most helpful to their development?

Homeschooling allows you to take full advantage of...everything around! When you see a need, you can fill it directly. No bureaucracy or paperwork. No pleading with administrators. You are in charge and you don't have to ask permission to give your children the best education.

The synergy from bringing all the good things together for your child multiplies the benefits exponentially.

For resources and downloads relating to Habit #6, go to:
https://the7successhabitsofhomeschoolers.com/habit6

Habit 7: Be a Model in Progress

Our deepest fear is not that we are inadequate. Our deepest fear is that we are powerful beyond measure. It is our light, not our darkness, that most frightens us. Your playing small does not serve the world. There is nothing enlightened about shrinking so that other people won't feel insecure around you. We are all meant to shine as children do. It's not just in some of us; it is in everyone. And as we let our lights shine, we unconsciously give other people permission to do the same. As we are liberated from our own fear, our presence automatically liberates others.

Kopite

You are busy. Maybe you're too busy. Perhaps you're even pulling your hair out. I hear you. Not only do you carry the usual responsibilities of parents, caring for the needs of home and family, but you have volunteered to accept full responsibility for the education of your children as well.

While to many of us, it just seems to be the logical extension of what we've been doing all along, it's a part of parenting that most parents in our culture largely turn over to the government. Say what you want about being involved in the schools (I've been there, too), but having your kids in your charge 365/24/7 is not the same as having them in supervised, (semi-) productive activities for seven hours per day, 180 days per year. It just isn't. Those 1,200 hours of "personal time" every year really add up.

But does that mean that as a stay-at-homeschooling mom or dad you are too busy to be a model of sound educational pursuits to your children? Too busy to improve? Too busy to be better, stronger, smarter? **No!**

Homeschooling is all about motivating your children to learn, to improve, to progress. How effective can you be if you do not **show** your children how important this is by your example? You must take time for all-around improvement. You must mentor life-long learning to your children. You, too, must "be all that you can be."

Unlike some homeschooling methods, I don't advocate that you must do exactly what you want your kids to do (oooing and ahing all the while) to motivate them to try. I did algebra three decades ago. I am not doing it six more times in order to "mentor" each of my children. Instead, model for them how to set goals and move forward. Start where you are. Get a little better every day. Make progress.

Don't let busyness become an excuse for inaction. Show your children how to accomplish in the face of obstacles...by doing it yourself. Find the time to set goals. And find the determination to complete them.

I Don't Have Time

With all you have to do, where can you find the time? Take a hard look at your life and activities. Do you see anywhere you can change or redirect? Can you cut out some nonessentials or become more efficient at the things you must do?

To get you started, ask yourself these questions. Answer them honestly. No one is looking.

Do you spend more time chatting, debating, or meme sharing with people on the internet whom you've never met than to your children and spouse?

In the interest of full disclosure, I begin with my own great vice. Back in the days before Al Gore invented the internet, in 1986, I was introduced to my first online chat experience. I was in college, had my first 512k Apple Macintosh, and found a local electronic bulletin board called Transporter. Live discussion through the computer. Amazing!

Next, there was America Online. My husband and I were such early adopters that we were "charter members" and got a spectacular lifelong discount deal. I came, first, to be on the staff in the Family Computing department and later for the Homeschooling Forum. I moderated message boards and organized chats. I even got a free, denim, AOL-logo embroidered shirt!

Next there were email listservs, newsgroups, moos, muds, major-domo, ftp, telnet, Archie, Jughead (Veronica, too), IRC, and gopher. And so much more. It was a brand-new world, waiting to be discovered (and invented).

Then there was the World Wide Web. [Pause as the music swells.] This brought blogs and message boards and later social media.

Can you say "cutting edge"? I was there. I was happening. I was wasting a lot of time.

Are there benefits to these venues? Absolutely. The speed and ready access of information is stunning.

Do they warrant the amount of time often afforded them? Usually not.

If you've got time to read and post on multiple sites, you might consider cutting back. (Unless it's my blog, of course.) You just might find time to do something really worthwhile.

Do you spend multiple hours per week staring at screens for entertainment?

One night a number of years ago, I was in the church gym, practicing my basketball skills with a handful of women who comprised our congregation's team. We were not highly skilled overall, but were getting a great workout and a good laugh. Suddenly, one of the women bolted to the door. "I have to go! ER is on!"

I was stunned.

Do you let a fictional TV show dictate how you deal with the real world? If you watch a TV show enough to know when it's on, you probably watch it enough that it interferes with your real life, as well. Give a good dose of consideration to the opportunity cost of sitting in front of the "boob tube." What are you giving up to do so? Is it worth it?

The last time I was this familiar with a television show schedule was in 1996, when a show called Early Edition was on. (You remember? The cat brought the newspaper a day early to the erstwhile hero?) In its defense, it was a really fun show with a great moral conscience. But now I honestly don't remember a single episode. (That's probably true for 99% of the television I've watched in my life.) You can be sure that the hours I spent watching could usually have been better used elsewhere. I probably could have published this book two decades earlier.

Even now, while entertainment scheduling is largely on-demand, we can still spend far too many hours idling away our time being amused.

The funny thing about this question is that no one is willing to admit it applies to them. When I ask the rhetorical question in convention speeches, it results in immediate, vigorous shaking of heads. And when I ask it online, it generates denials. So, I have no idea who is watching all the TV that gets watched but apparently, it's no one I have ever met. Whenever a homeschooler posts to a group, describing their outrage at the latest episode of Oprah, it's always prefaced with, "I really never, ever watch Oprah, but I just happened to be flipping through the channels—looking for some valuable educational programming—the other day when Oprah happened to be on and…"

My less-than-stellar impression of Oprah Winfrey aside, we should at least note that she attained success by taking action, not by sitting on the couch watching someone else do it.

So, if you are the one watching all the recorded television hours for everyone else, admit it! Then see if you can reduce the watching just a bit to squeeze in a little serious self-improvement.

Do you spend more time creating memory pages to chronicle an event than you actually spent living the event?

You already know I hate crafts. So, maybe this is just a pot shot at the world's most popular hobby. But I really don't get it. The appetite for newer, better ways to archive moments that no one really cares about seems insatiable.

The time, money, storage space, all-night sleepovers in community recreation centers to "crop till you drop"—is this really the dream life you envisioned? Is gluing unidentifiable ornamentation onto oversized, textured paper really the best there is in your future? At least take a minute or two to identify the possible alternatives.

I have a hard time completely hating crafts. Many of my children love them. Most women I know would prefer crafting to anything except chocolate. A good friend from high school is the founding editor of the world's largest scrapbooking magazine. (This has the distinctly unpleasant side effect of turning every "old gang" luncheon into an I'm-behind-in-my-scrapbooks confession session. With the pleasant side effect being that I always make everyone else look good.)

If you love scrapbooking or any other crafty, kitschy hobby, more power to you. But I'm confident that anyone who "invests" in crafting does have time do something else once in a while. At least stop to think of all the good you can do in the world and decide if crafting is the best of the best.

I'm sure there are people who are truly so busy, that they can't take on any more. But without exception, these are the people who are accomplishing incredible things that put the rest of us to shame.

You have the time. Do you have the desire?

The Success System

We are to be a light on the hill. We are busy, but not so busy that we can put our light under a bushel. We are meant to shine.

And how do we shine? By discovering our ideal lives and our best selves and moving toward them.

What is your dream life? If you don't know where you want to go, someone or something else will decide for you. If you don't actively determine where your life is headed, your children, your spouse, your neighbors, your church, the TV, the clock, your habits—something will still occupy all 24 hours of your day.

Rather than live life passively at the whim of other people and things, decide, consciously, where your days are going to take you. Make a plan to live your dreams!

Master Goal List

Get a few pieces of lined paper. Divide them each into two, long columns. Each column should have 101 rows. Why 101? One hundred is a very tidy number, but this is not a tidy list. This is a list that you will add to for the rest of your life. When you see that there are 101 lines, I want you to remember vividly that this list is not done until you die (hopefully from exhilaration, not boredom). This is your lifelong bucket list.

In the first column, begin to list everything you ever want to be or do or have before you die. Everything. No holds barred. Nothing held back. No equivocation. Don't be shy or reserved. Don't limit your options. Be bold in declaring what you want for your life.

Write each of these items as if they already exist as you dream them. Don't write, "I am going to lose weight." Write, "I am fit and strong." Don't list things that are impossible (like sprouting wings), but do list things that seem unreasonable (like donating $1,000,000 to charity). Go.

Harder than you thought, wasn't it? I find that the first 15 are easy for most people. 30 is starting to drag. It might take a couple of days of thought to get through 90. Getting to 101 can be like pulling teeth. Stick with it anyway.

When you're done, in the second column, write down the thing that is keeping you from achieving that particular goal—the limiting factors, the barriers. What is holding you back? What makes this so hard to change?

Write it as a positive expression, as if it's already extinguished. Write it with the understanding that it's a barrier that you will no longer tolerate in your life. Don't write, "I eat too many potato chips." Write, "I only feed my body with fresh, healthy food."

When you have this massive master list complete, you're going to tear it apart. Literally. Cut each item into a strip of paper. Now you are going to categorize your goals. Place each strip in a pile, by type. Here are the seven categories I suggest:

- **Body Goals**: health; fitness; beauty; clothing

- **Fun Goals**: travel; leisure; recreation; adventure

- **Good Goals**: spirituality; character; service; philanthropy

- **Home Goals**: design; décor; organization; cleaning

- **Love Goals**: marriage; family; relationships; community

- **Mind Goals**: education; training; productivity; skills

- **Money Goals**: career; budgeting; investment; retirement

Don't anguish over this. Don't lose sleep. It doesn't have to be perfect. Take no more than five seconds per goal. In less than ten minutes, you're done.

Look over your goal piles. Are they balanced? Do you have lots of goals for your home/organization and few for health/fitness? Do you overemphasize finances and ignore spirituality?

If so, spend a few days thinking about the areas you **might** be neglecting and how you can add some appropriate level of balance to fit with your values. They categories don't need to be identical. Family is probably more important to you than leisure (you are homeschooling, after all). But it's good to look at our lives in a quantifiable way, to see if improvements should be made. If you think your life is unbalanced, make a few changes.

Now create a new list for each of the goal areas and write down every goal that ended up in the corresponding pile.

Now you have your own Master Goal List. From now on, whenever you think of anything you want to do (or be or have), add it to the appropriate category list.

To download a Master Goal List page to use, go to my web.

Choose Your Most Compelling Goal

With your goals clearly listed in black and white, it's time to break them down from huge life dreams into manageable chunks.

Choose one goal from your master list that you are going to work on. Just one. Choose the one that is most important—the one that will make the biggest, single impact on your life and provide the greatest positive change if accomplished. (Again, don't get anxiety over this selection. If it's too hard to decide with this criterion, pick something in your top ten.)

Write this goal on a new piece of paper. Under the goal, write a paragraph explaining why it is so important to you. What will you gain if you accomplish it? What will you lose if you don't? Be very specific.

Now read the paragraph aloud. Is your paragraph compelling? If not, rewrite it. If it's not compelling to you, you won't go through the difficulty to accomplish it. But if your reason to do it—your "why"—is compelling enough, you are likely to figure out the "how" to get to the finish line.

Goals Become Projects

Next you need to figure out how you will move forward. It might be obvious and simple. But it might require research and study. You may need to read or consult a mentor to find the action steps. If this is the case, your first action is to find out what the next steps will be.

Once you know how to proceed, write down an action plan. Break the process into an itemized list. Whenever possible, make the steps so simple—so ridiculously doable—that you would feel silly for not doing them. Tiny baby steps are great motivators.

Most of us have what I would call "rotating resolutions." We write down a bunch of exciting goals for the upcoming year and then, upon the expiration of that year, we simply move the old goals to a new page, since none of them were accomplished.

How many different times have you resolved to lose ten pounds or put money into your savings account? How many times did you actually accomplish it?

A friend of mine always made a list of New Year's resolutions a mile long. To most of us that would just mean a long list of failures. But, instead, he accomplished almost all of them every single year. His secret? Each goal was tiny. One year, for example, he set the goal to "pray more on my knees and less in the car." It didn't take long to check that off.

Is accomplishing a tiny goal a big deal? Perhaps not individually. But myriad tiny goals add up. They accumulate into more than most of us do in a decade of writing down overwhelming resolutions—and then rolling them over to the next year, unaccomplished.

Another example of the power of very doable goals occurred years ago in a church meeting. One of my ecclesiastical leaders challenged the entire congregation, "This year, I ask each of you to read your scriptures for 15 seconds each day."

That brought a good laugh, but taught me an invaluable principle. How many of us, in good faith, could claim that we didn't have a spare 15 second daily to follow that counsel? Many in that meeting started to read their scriptures regularly because they knew they could commit to 15 seconds. And, of course, most of them read more than that. Mission accomplished.

Projects Become Actions

With your goal broken down into a step-by-step project, you are ready to take action!

Get a new piece of paper and make a Next Actions list. Go back to your project page and find the very first step to reach your goal. Write it down on your Next Actions list. If possible, create some momentum by taking that step right now. Now you're on the right track, moving forward, and ready to keep going.

As soon as you finish an action item, check it off. Then add the next step from the project to your list. Keep this list handy. You'll always be aware of what you need to do next without being overwhelmed by the many steps to completion.

Repeat each action item until the goal is complete. Keep it updated and keep moving toward your ultimate goal.

Can You Do More?

If moving forward on one project is all you can handle, then just keep moving forward until it's done. When it's done, choose another project with a big impact and follow the steps above. If it makes sense, choose a goal from a different category than the first, so that you can improve in all areas of your life. But always consider the one with the greatest impact.

If you find you can work on more than one goal at a time, choose another goal project and work through it simultaneously with the first.

I try to have one active goal from each category at all times, when possible. That provides some variety, motivation, and a sense of accomplishment. Sometimes, however, it makes sense to focus on fewer goals more intensely. See what works for you.

Quest for Perfection

Face it. You are not perfect. No one is. And you are not expected to be.

The goal is not to have a perfect face, perfect body, perfect nails, perfect home, perfect garden, perfect children, perfect bank account, and a perfect husband. (Sorry, the last is already taken, anyway).

The goal is to have constant forward **momentum**. Get a little better every day. Move closer to that dream life. The joy is in the journey. And the consistent, forward movement is what serves as the best role model for your children.

I'm not just talking about goals that are focused on homeschooling or strictly related to what we think of when we discuss "formal education." I'm talking about improving in all areas of life. Anything positive and good that you do to become better, smarter, healthier, happier, wealthier, more helpful, more organized, or closer to your potential is a good example to your children. And it's a renewal process that will make homeschooling—and everything else—better.

In early 2004 I got a call from an old high school friend named Jill.

"Alison, let's celebrate our 40th birthdays by running a marathon together!"

Yea, that sounds much better than cramming my face with chocolate cake and ice cream and getting a pedicure. Sure.

I had just given birth to my last child and was in no mood—or shape—to run 26.2 miles. But in the back of my subconscious, a little voice reminded me that I had written "run a marathon" on my master goal list in 1987—when I was only 23.

Truth is, I didn't really want to run a marathon. I like dancing, sports, even race-walking, but I hate running. Mostly I wanted to be able tell other people that I had run a marathon. I wanted to be cool. I wanted bragging rights. And I wanted to cross the darned goal off my list!

And if I didn't do it in 2004, when would I? On my 80th birthday?

So, I relented. Then I panicked. I looked for others to join my misery and recruited my husband and my sister to join me. I had no idea where to begin, so I looked up a marathon-training schedule in *Runner's World*.

I trained for almost five miserable months, and then drove with my posse to Logan, Utah, for the Top of Utah Marathon.

After the carbo-load the night before (without a doubt, my favorite part of marathoning), we hunkered down for the night, prepared for a very early morning. When the alarm went off, we ate half a peanut butter bagel, decked ourselves out in Coolmax, packed our fanny packs with Gu and band-aids, and headed out for the crash site.

Once there—surrounded mostly by real runners and feeling obese and out of place—we boarded the busses. Then we drove from the loading point at the finish line, to the starting line. And we drove and drove and drove. Realizing that every minute of driving was equivalent to about 14 hours of running, I got nauseous and more anxious by the minute.

"What have I done? What was I thinking? I'll never make it! I am a total idiot!"

It was reminiscent of my college pageant days, standing on the stage as names are called—""...and third runner-up goes to..."—becoming more and more sure you won't even win Miss Congeniality and wanting to disappear into the stage floor.

When we finally arrived at the starting point—approximately 2,000 miles from where we boarded the busses—I was babbling and delirious. Sam and Nora were ready. Jill looked like an Olympian. I was ready to be committed.

Some jittery minutes later, the race started. I pulled back, easing in with the slow crowd to avoid being trampled. I sidled up to the one woman in the crowd who—based entirely on appearances—did not intimidate me to death. She was at least in her mid-fifties, was about five feet tall and probably just as wide. I was sure she would have cardiac arrest during the event and I wanted to be able to make her last wishes known.

But within about 30 seconds of jog/chat I found that she was a member of the 50 States Marathon Club. The members of this club commit to run one marathon in each state in the USA. She was on marathon 36. Holy cow.

If she could do it, why couldn't I?

Hour after hour I plodded along. I saw dozens of people drop out, but kept on going. Just me and my iPod.

At mile 13, I was feeling pretty good, but by mile 21, my legs turned into wooden logs, each step jarring through my whole body. I thought I would die. But "Old Lady 50" kept me going. At mile 23, my husband—long finished and rested—drove back on the route to find me. He drove beside me for a number of miles, handing me water and giving encouragement.

At mile 26.1, I sprinted the last tenth of a mile toward the finish line. Exhilarated!

I beat Old Lady 50—but only by about four minutes. (First impressions are often very wrong!) And of those who finished, I was only ahead of a handful. But I finished. I finished!

Physically it's the hardest thing I've ever done. And though I didn't make my mark in racing history, it's one of the accomplishments I am most proud of, because it took so much out of me. And I didn't quit.

You don't need to be a model of perfection—just make sure you aren't a model of stagnation. You need to be a model of progress in all areas of your life.

It can be slow progress. It can be miniscule progress. It can be progress by baby steps. It can be last-place-of-all progress. It can be progress that is barely visible.

It's the direction, not the velocity that counts. Keep setting goals. Keep improving. Keep moving forward. **Be a model in progress.**

Life is not a journey to the grave with the intention of arriving safely in a pretty and well-preserved body, but rather to skid in broadside, thoroughly used up, totally worn out, and loudly proclaiming, "WOW! What a ride!"

Hunter S. Thompson

Final Thoughts

You were already busy. Then you took charge of educating your children, too. Your life will have to go on the back burner for now. Right? Wrong!

Do you want your children to think they are working hard, getting educated, learning so much, just so they can have children and stop doing everything? Do you want them to think their purpose in life is to become educated only so they can stop all progress to educate their children... and then the cycle continues generation after generation?

It may seem daunting at first, but remember that you will always be a mentor for your children. What they see is what "normal" looks like. Lifelong learning, progress, and contributions is a great "normal" for them to see.

Like everything else, being a model in progress doesn't have to be a sprint. Start where you are today and move forward as you are able. Some days that's less, some days that's more. But keep moving forward. The progress accumulates!

**For resources and downloads relating to Habit #7, go to:
https://the7successhabitsofhomeschoolers.com/habit7**

Press On!

What are you going to do with your one wild and precious life?

Mary Oliver

I used to say, "I do not believe that homeschooling is the 'right' way—or the 'righteous' way—to educate children." But I've changed my mind. I believe it is the only sound way to educate children. And I believe if you aren't doing it, you are almost certainly short-changing your children.

Homeschooling isn't about location. It's about authority. Who's in charge? Is it a federal regulation, the school board, the principal, the PTA, a randomly-assigned teacher? Or is it you and your child?

If we look properly at the available educational opportunities, we will see the public schools as a resource, but never as the only source. They are merely one choice in the smorgasbord, one we will choose only if it is the best available, given our particular situation. All other resources should be similarly viewed—and analyzed—to determine if they are the best way to meet the needs of our amazingly unique children.

Learning to open our vision of what education can be is a difficult step for many of us who grew up with only one educational model. To us, "school" starts when we're five and ends when we're 18. It begins at 8:00 am, after a bus ride to school, and ends at 3:00 pm with a bus ride home. In between, we spend 180 days per year with less than four absences and five tardies, studying a predetermined set of requirements, rotated in scheduled intervals, broken up by a 23-minute lunch period and five, seven-minute transfer times. (Except on assembly days, when the A schedule is replaced by the C schedule and 4th period comes 2nd, directly after 5th and class changes are allowed 4.5 minutes with lunch schedules shifted a half hour and the milk line is replaced by entrée number two from the previous Tuesday.) For some of us, it's really hard to let all of that go.

Changing your mindset may seem overwhelming and impossible. It isn't—it is just unfamiliar. And the key to dealing with the unfamiliar is to acquire a roadmap to guide you through the sometimes-murky waters of educating your own children.

Now, after homeschooling for 26 years— having sent off my five graduates to private universities (including some academic and talent scholarships, currently with three bachelor's and one master's degree among them) and on religious missions—and embarking on my 27th and final year with our youngest son, the most common statements made to me are:

1. "I would love to homeschool my children, but I could never do it!"

2. "I just don't have the patience!"

3. "How can you stand having them all at home all day long?"

I smile. I wouldn't have it any other way.